I0285435

BREADLESS SANDWICHES, WRAPS AND BURGERS

100 DELICIOUS NO-BREAD SANDWICHES, WRAPS AND BURGERS

MILTON CUMMINGS

All rights reserved.

Disclaimer

The information contained in this eBook is meant to serve as a comprehensive collection of strategies that the author of this eBook has done research about. Summaries, strategies, tips and tricks are only recommendation by the author, and reading this eBook will not guarantee that one's results will exactly mirror the author's results. The author of the eBook has made all reasonable effort to provide current and accurate information for the readers of the eBook. The author and its associates will not be held liable for any unintentional error or omissions that may be found. The material in the eBook may include information by third parties. Third party materials comprise of opinions expressed by their owners. As such, the author of the eBook does not assume responsibility or liability for any third party material or opinions. Whether because of the progression of the internet, or the unforeseen changes in company policy and editorial submission guidelines, what is stated as fact at the time of this writing may become outdated or inapplicable later.

The eBook is copyright © 2022 with all rights reserved. It is illegal to redistribute, copy, or create derivative work from this eBook whole or in part. No parts of this report may be reproduced or retransmitted in any reproduced or retransmitted in any forms whatsoever without the writing expressed and signed permission from the author.

TABLE OF CONTENTS

TABLE OF CONTENTS 3

INTRODUCTION 7

SANDWICHES 8

   1. CAULIFLOWER GRILLED CHEESE.. 9
   2. INDIAN NO BREAD SANDWICH 12
   3. CURRIED SHRIMP-STACKED TOMATOES.. 15
   4. TURKEY SLIDERS WITH SWEET POTATO.. 17
   5. HASSEL BACK TOMATO CLUBS 20
   6. FRIED GREEN NAPOLEONS WITH COLESLAW... 22
   7. RICOTTA-STUFFED PORTOBELLO MUSHROOMS 25
   8. APPLE AND PEANUT BUTTER STACKERS 28
   9. FRIED GREEN TOMATOES.. 30
   10. CUCUMBER SUBS... 33
   11. BAKED EGGPLANT SANDWICHES.. 35
   12. THE NO-BREAD BLT 38
   13. BREADLESS ITALIAN SUB SANDWICH 41
   14. APPLE, HAM, AND CHEESE SANDWICHES 44
   15. BREADLESS RED PEPPER SANDWICH 46
   16. SWEET POTATO BURGER BUNS... 48
   17. TUNA PICKLE BOATS 50
   18. GRILLED PORTOBELLO BURGERS.. 52
   19. BURGERS WITH TOFU 55
   20. PORTABELLA AND HALLOUMI BURGERS... 58
   21. TUNA SALAD SANDWICHES WITH CUCUMBER... 61
   22. MEDITERRANEAN WRAP WITH TOFU OR CHICKEN... 64
   23. HAM AND CHEESE SANDWICH 67
   24. SWISS CHARD WRAP WITH PESTO... 71

BURGERS 74

   25. CHICKEN SUSHI BURGER 75
   26. TOMATO AVOCADO BURGERS 82
   27. RED BEET BURGERS WITH ARUGULA.. 85

28. Macadamia-Cashew Patties 88
29. Pecan-Lentil Burgers 91
30. Black Bean Burgers 94
31. Some-Kind of-Nut Burgers 97
32. Golden Veggie Burgers 100
33. White Bean and Walnut Patties 103
34. Curried Chickpea Patties 106
35. Pinto Bean Patties with Mayo 109
36. Vegan Veggie burger 112
37. Garbanzo bean burgers 114
38. Bulgur patties 116
39. All-star veggie patty 118
40. Oatmeal veggie patty 120
41. Bulgur Lentil veggie patty 123
42. Veggie patties 125
43. Mushroom tofu patty 128
44. Ovo veggie patty 131
45. Quick veggie patties 133
46. TexMex veggie patty 135
47. Veggie bean patties 138
48. Veggie oat burgers 140
49. Walnut and veggie patties 142
50. Wild mushroom patty 144
51. Wonderful veggie patties 147
52. Lentil rice patties 149
53. Bean and corn patties 151
54. Black Bean Grillers 154
55. Vegan Bacon patties 157
56. Barley Oat patties 160
57. Tempeh patties 162

WRAPS AND ROLLS 165

58. No Bread Turkey Club 166
59. Collard Wraps with Quinoa and Sweet Potato 169
60. Copycat in N' Out Burger 172
61. Carrot and Spinach Wrap 175
62. Vegan Mediterranean Wraps 177
63. Chickpea hummus wraps 180

64. Baby Beet Wraps 182
65. Vegan Shawarma 184
66. Chipotle Tofu Rainbow Wraps 187
67. Seared Portobello Fajitas 190
68. Beer-Marinated Seitan Fajitas 192
69. Seitan Tacos 195
70. Refried Bean and Salsa Quesadillas 197
71. Spinach, Mushroom, and Black Bean Quesadillas 199
72. Black Bean and Corn Burritos 202
73. Red Bean Burritos 204
74. Ham and cheese cucumber roll ups 206
75. Crispy Salami Roll-ups 209
76. Italian Beef Wrappers 211
77. Italian Pepperoni Roll-ups 213
78. Appetizer Tortilla Pinwheels 216
79. Crispy vegan rolls 218
80. Vegan stuffed cabbage rolls 221
81. Vegan nori rolls 224
82. Mediterranean Rolls 227
83. Avocado Spring Rolls 230
84. Vegetarian Spring Roll 232
85. Vegetarian cabbage rolls 235
86. Vegetarian egg rolls 238
87. Vegetarian Thai spring rolls 240
88. Unstuffed cabbage rolls 243
89. Vegetarian summer roll 245
90. Curried Tofu "Egg Salad" Pitas 248

SANDWICH/BURGER SPREADS 251

91. Sun-dried tomatoes Spread 252
92. Hummus dreams 254
93. Avocado love 256
94. Pimiento spread for sandwich filling 258
95. Tofu sandwich spread 260
96. Veggie sandwich spread 262
97. Easy "Tofuna" Sandwich Spread 264
98. Indian lentil spread 266
99. Chickpea sandwich spread 268

100. Curried bean spread 270

CONCLUSION **272**

INTRODUCTION

I think it's safe to say that most people think of bread when craving a sandwich. Whether loaded with meat or piled high with veggies, one thing that mostly stays the same is the fact that all the yummy fillings are held together by bread. However, many people are looking for new ways to enjoy their favorite burger or sandwich, minus the bread, without sacrificing flavor.

These delightful sandwich recipes have all kinds of crafty ways to make satisfying sandwiches without the use of traditional bread. Whether you're just looking for something new, gluten-free, or Paleo, we've got the best non-bread sandwiches for your taste buds. It is time that you treat yourself to a satisfying bite without feeling guilty or deprived of regular bread. Not to mention, you can mix-and-match bread alternatives with all of the recipes included in this book. The possibilities are endless!

SANDWICHES

1. Cauliflower Grilled Cheese

yield: 2 SANDWICHES

Ingredients

- 1 medium cauliflower head, riced
- 1 large egg
- $\frac{1}{2}$ cup grated Parmesan cheese
- 1 teaspoon dried basil or Italian herb seasoning
- 2 thick slices white cheddar cheese

Directions

a) Place the riced cauliflower in a microwave safe bowl and microwave on high for 2 minutes. Then remove the cauliflower from the microwave, stir and microwave again for 3 minutes.

b) Repeat this step again and microwave for 4 minutes.

c) Remove the cauliflower from the microwave, stir for the last time and set in the microwave for another 4-5 minutes. The key is to get really nice and dry cauliflower rice.

d) Next, combine the riced cauliflower with egg, parmesan, and dried basil and stir to combine.

e) Preheat your oven to 350F. Line a baking sheet with parchment paper.

f) Divide the cauliflower mix into four portions and shape each portion on a baking sheet, to 1/3-inch thick rectangle.

g) Bake for 15 minutes or until golden brown. Cool the cauliflower slices on a wire rack.

h) Next top two slices with the cheese. Sandwich with the remaining slices and pop under a broiler. Broil for 3-4 minutes or until the cheese is melted.

2. Indian no bread sandwich

Servings 6

Ingredients

- 1 cup semolina (coarse)
- ½ cup curd
- 1 teaspoon chili flakes
- ½ teaspoons salt
- ½ cup water
- ½ carrot (finely chopped)
- ½ onion (finely chopped)
- 2 Tablespoons sweet corn
- ½ capsicum (finely chopped)
- 1 Tablespoons coriander (finely chopped)
- ½ teaspoons salt
- butter (for greasing)
- 1 cheese slice (quartered)

Directions

a) firstly, in a large bowl take 1 cup semolina, ½ cup curd, 1 teaspoons chilli flakes and ½ teaspoons salt.

b) mix well making sure everything is well combined.

c) now add ½ cup water and combine well.

d) add ½ carrot, ½ onion, 2 Tablespoons sweet corn, ½ capsicum and 1 Tablespoons coriander.

e) mix well forming a thick batter.

f) rest for 10 minutes or until the semolina absorbs water.

g) further, add ¼ cup water and mix well forming a smooth batter.

h) now grease the sandwich maker with some butter.

i) just before preparing a sandwich, add ½ teaspoons salt and mix gently.

j) once the batter turns frothy, transfer a Tablespoons of batter to the sandwich maker.

k) place a cheese slice. make sure the cheese slice is the size of the sandwich.

l) cover with the batter making sure it is uniformly covered.

m) now close the lid of the sandwich maker and press tight.

n) grill until the sandwich turns golden brown and is cooked uniformly.

o) finally, enjoy no bread sandwich with tomato sauce.

3. Curried Shrimp-Stacked Tomatoes

Makes 4 servings

Ingredients

- 4 large heirloom tomatoes
- 6 tablespoons reduced-fat mayonnaise
- 1 teaspoon curry powder
- 1/4 teaspoon salt
- 1/4 teaspoon ground ginger
- 3/4 pound peeled and deveined cooked shrimp (61-70 per pound)
- 1 celery rib, chopped
- 1/2 cup finely chopped cucumber
- 1 small navel orange, peeled and finely chopped
- 2 green onions, thinly sliced

Directions

a) Trim and cut each tomato into three thick slices; drain on paper towels.

b) In a large bowl, mix mayonnaise and seasonings; stir in remaining ingredients. For each serving, stack three slices tomatoes, layering with shrimp mixture.

4. Turkey Sliders with Sweet Potato

Makes 10 servings

Ingredients

- 4 Applewood-smoked bacon strips, finely chopped
- 1-pound ground turkey
- 1/2 cup panko crumbs
- 2 large eggs
- 1/2 cup grated Parmesan cheese
- 4 tablespoons chopped fresh cilantro
- 1 teaspoon dried basil
- 1/2 teaspoon ground cumin
- 1 tablespoon soy sauce
- 2 large sweet potatoes
- Shredded Colby-Monterey Jack cheese

Directions

a) In a large skillet, cook bacon over medium heat until crisp; drain on paper towels. Discard all but 2 tablespoons drippings. Set skillet aside. Combine bacon with next 8 ingredients until well mixed; cover and refrigerate at least 30 minutes.

b) Preheat oven to 425°. Cut sweet potatoes into 20 slices about 1/2 in. thick. Place slices on an ungreased baking sheet; bake until sweet potatoes are tender but not mushy, 30-35 minutes. Remove slices; cool on a wire rack.

c) Heat skillet with reserved drippings over medium-high heat. Shape turkey mixture into slider-sized patties. Cook sliders in batches, 3-4 minutes on each side, taking care not to crowd skillet. Add a pinch of shredded cheddar after flipping each slider the first time. Cook until a thermometer reads 165° and juices run clear.

d) To serve, place each slider on a sweet potato slice; dab with honey Dijon mustard. Cover with a second sweet potato slice. Pierce with toothpick.

5. Hassel back Tomato Clubs

Makes 2 servings

Ingredients

- 4 plum tomatoes
- 2 slices Swiss cheese, quartered
- 4 cooked bacon strips, halved
- 4 slices deli turkey
- 4 Bibb lettuce leaves
- 1/2 medium ripe avocado, peeled and cut into 8 slices
- Cracked pepper

Directions

a) Cut 4 crosswise slices in each tomato, leaving them intact at the bottom.

b) Fill each slice with cheese, bacon, turkey, lettuce and avocado. Sprinkle with pepper.

6. Fried Green Napoleons with Coleslaw

Ingredients

- 1/3 cup mayonnaise
- 1/4 cup white vinegar
- 2 tablespoons sugar
- 1 teaspoon salt
- 1 teaspoon garlic powder
- 1/2 teaspoon pepper
- 1 package (14 ounces) three-color coleslaw mix
- 1/4 cup finely chopped onion
- 1 can (11 ounces) mandarin oranges, drained
- fried tomatoes:
- 1 large egg, lightly beaten
- Dash hot pepper sauce, or to taste
- 1/4 cup all-purpose flour
- 1 cup dry crumbs
- 2 medium green tomatoes, cut into 4 slices each
- Oil for frying
- 1/2 teaspoon salt
- 1/4 teaspoon pepper

- 1/2 cup refrigerated pimiento cheese
- 4 teaspoons pepper jelly

Directions

a) Combine first six ingredients. Add coleslaw mix and onion. Add mandarin oranges; stir carefully.

b) In a shallow bowl, whisk egg and hot sauce. Place flour and crumbs in separate shallow bowls. Dip tomato slices in flour to coat both sides; shake off excess. Dip in egg mixture, then in crumbs, patting to help coating adhere.

c) In an electric skillet or deep fryer, heat oil to 350°. Fry tomato slices, a few at a time, until browned, 1-2 minutes on each side. Drain on paper towels. Sprinkle with salt and pepper.

d) To assemble napoleons, layer one tomato slice with 1 tablespoon pimiento cheese. Repeat layers. Top with 1 teaspoon pepper jelly. Repeat with remaining tomato slices. Serve over coleslaw.

7. Ricotta-Stuffed Portobello Mushrooms

Ingredients

- 3/4 cup reduced-fat ricotta cheese
- 3/4 cup grated Parmesan cheese, divided
- 1/2 cup shredded part-skim mozzarella cheese
- 2 tablespoons minced fresh parsley
- 1/8 teaspoon pepper
- 6 large Portobello mushrooms
- 6 slices large tomato
- 3/4 cup fresh basil leaves
- 3 tablespoons slivered almonds or pine nuts, toasted
- 1 small garlic clove
- 2 tablespoons olive oil
- 2 to 3 teaspoons water

Directions

a) In a small bowl, mix ricotta cheese, 1/4 cup Parmesan cheese, mozzarella cheese, parsley and pepper. Remove and discard stems from mushrooms; with a spoon, scrape and remove gills. Fill caps with ricotta mixture. Top with tomato slices.

b) Grill, covered, over medium heat until mushrooms are tender, 8-10 minutes. Remove from grill with a metal spatula.

c) Meanwhile, place basil, almonds and garlic in a small food processor; pulse until chopped. Add remaining Parmesan cheese; pulse just until blended. While processing, gradually add oil and enough water to reach desired consistency. Spoon over stuffed mushrooms before serving.

8. Apple and Peanut Butter Stackers

Ingredients

- 2 medium apples
- 1/3 cup chunky peanut butter
- Optional fillings: granola, miniature semisweet chocolate chips

Directions

a) Core apples. Cut each apple crosswise into six slices. Spread peanut butter over six slices; sprinkle with fillings of your choice.

b) Top with remaining apple slices.

9. Fried Green Tomatoes

Ingredients

- 1/4 cup fat-free mayonnaise
- 1/4 teaspoon grated lime zest
- 2 tablespoons lime juice
- 1 teaspoon minced fresh thyme or 1/4 teaspoon dried thyme
- 1/2 teaspoon pepper, divided
- 1/4 cup all-purpose flour
- 2 large egg whites, lightly beaten
- 3/4 cup cornmeal
- 1/4 teaspoon salt
- 2 medium green tomatoes
- 2 medium red tomatoes
- 2 tablespoons canola oil
- 8 slices Canadian bacon

Directions

a) Mix the first 4 ingredients and 1/4 teaspoon pepper; refrigerate until serving. Place flour in a shallow bowl; place egg whites in a separate shallow bowl. In a third bowl, mix cornmeal, salt and remaining pepper.

b) Cut each tomato crosswise into 4 slices. Dredge 1 slice in flour to lightly coat; shake off excess. Dip in egg whites, then in cornmeal mixture. Repeat with remaining tomato slices.

c) In a large nonstick skillet, heat oil over medium heat. In batches, cook tomatoes until golden brown, 4-5 minutes per side.

d) In same pan, lightly brown Canadian bacon on both sides. For each, stack 1 slice each green tomato, bacon and red tomato. Serve with sauce.

10.   Cucumber Subs

SERVES 2

Ingredients

- 2 medium to large cucumbers
- deli meat-turkey, ham, or other deli meat slices or shaved
- bacon (optional)
- green onions (optional)
- tomatoes (optional)
- any sandwich fillers (optional)
- laughing cow cheese or mayo or cream cheese or any other condiment

Directions

a) Cut the cucumber length-wise, from tip to tip. Scoop out the inside of the cucumber to make room for your sandwich fillers. Add meat, veggies, and other sandwich makings to the inside of the cucumber.

b) Place one half of the cucumber on the other half. Enjoy!!

11. **Baked Eggplant Sandwiches**

Servings: 4

Ingredients

- 1 teaspoon olive oil
- 2 eggs
- ½ cup all-purpose flour, or more as needed
- salt and freshly ground black pepper to taste
- 1 pinch cayenne pepper, or more to taste
- 1 cup panko crumbs
- 8 slices of eggplant, cut 3/8 inch thick
- 2 slices provolone cheese, cut into quarters
- 12 thin slices salami
- 2 ⅔ tablespoons olive oil, divided
- 2 ⅔ tablespoons finely grated Parmigiano-Reggiano cheese, divided

Directions

a) Preheat oven to 425 degrees F (220 degrees C). Line a baking sheet with aluminum foil.

b) Beat eggs in a small, shallow bowl. Mix flour, salt, black pepper, and cayenne pepper in a large shallow dish. Pour panko crumbs in another large shallow dish.

c) Top one slice of eggplant with 1/4 slice provolone cheese, 3 slices salami, and 1/4 slice provolone cheese. Place an equally-sized slice of eggplant on top. Repeat with remaining eggplant slices, cheese, and salami.

d) Gently press each eggplant sandwich into the seasoned flour to coat; shake off excess. Dip both sides of each sandwich into beaten egg, then press into panko crumbs. Place on the prepared baking sheet while you make the remaining eggplant sandwiches.

e) Drizzle 1 teaspoon olive oil in a circle about 3 inches in diameter onto the foil; place an eggplant sandwich onto the oiled area. Sprinkle about 1 teaspoon Parmigiano-Reggiano cheese over the sandwich. Repeat with remaining 3 sandwiches, drizzling an area on the foil with olive oil, placing a sandwich onto the oil, and topping with Parmesan cheese. Drizzle tops of each sandwich with 1 teaspoon olive oil.

f) Bake in the preheated oven for 10 minutes. Flip sandwiches and sprinkle 1 teaspoon Parmigiano-Reggiano cheese onto the top. Bake until browned and a paring knife inserts easily into the eggplant, 8 to 10 more minutes. Serve warm or at room temperature.

12.   The No-Bread BLT

yield: 1 SERVING

Ingredients

- 6 slices bacon, cut in half horizontally
- lettuce leaves
- fresh tomato, sliced

Directions

a) Place three slices next to each other in a vertical row on a baking tray lined with a silicone mat.

b) Flap the top of the outer two slices down, then place a slice of bacon horizontally across them.

c) Flap the bacon back up, then flap up the central slice, and place another horizontal slice in the middle. Then add the final horizontal slice at the bottom by flapping up the two outer slices.

d) Repeat to form another bacon weave (you will need two per BLT).

e) Place an inverted non-stick rack over the top of the bacon and cook under a preheated broiler until the bacon starts to go crispy. Remove the rack, and flip over the bacon. Return to the broiler if necessary.

f) Transfer the bacon weaves to kitchen paper to drain the excess fat.

g) Add sliced tomato and crunchy romaine lettuce to one bacon weave, then top with the second weave.

13.   Breadless Italian Sub Sandwich

Yield: 4 sandwiches

Ingredients

- 8 large Portobello mushrooms, wiped clean
- 2 tablespoons extra-virgin olive oil
- Kosher salt
- 1 tablespoon red wine vinegar
- 1 tablespoon finely chopped pepperoncini with seeds
- 1/2 teaspoon dried oregano
- Freshly ground black pepper
- 2 ounces sliced provolone (about 4 slices)
- 2 ounces thinly sliced low-sodium ham (about 4 slices)
- 1 ounce thinly sliced Genoa salami (about 4 slices)
- 1 small tomato, cut into 4 slices
- 1/2 cup shredded iceberg lettuce
- 4 pimento-stuffed olives

Directions

a) Position an oven rack in the top third of the oven and preheat the oven broiler.

b) Remove the stems from the mushrooms and discard. Lay the mushroom caps gill-side-up and use a sharp knife to completely remove the gills (so that the caps will lie flat).

c) Arrange the mushroom caps on a baking sheet, brush all over with 1 tablespoon of oil and sprinkle with 1/4 teaspoon salt. Broil until the caps are just tender, flipping halfway through, 4 to 5 minutes per side. Allow to cool completely.

d) Whisk together the vinegar, pepperoncini, oregano, remaining 1 tablespoon oil and a few grinds of black pepper in a small bowl.

e) Assemble the sandwiches: Arrange one mushroom cap, cut side-up, on a work surface. Fold 1 piece of provolone to fit on top of the cap and repeat with 1 slice each of ham and salami.

f) Top with 1 slice of tomato and about 2 tablespoons of lettuce. Drizzle with some of the pepperoncini vinaigrette. Sandwich with another mushroom cap and secure with a toothpick threaded with an olive. Repeat with the remaining ingredients to make 3 more sandwiches.

g) Wrap each sandwich halfway in wax paper (this will help catch all the juices) and serve.

14. Apple, Ham, and Cheese Sandwiches

Servings: 2

Ingredients

- apple
- Ham slices
- Colby Jack Slices
- Brown Mustard, Dijon style or condiment of choice

Directions

a) Slice apples into rings.

b) Add Ham slices. Top with cheese slices.

c) Spread mustard on the top ring of the sandwich and place on top (condiment side down).

15.   Breadless Red Pepper Sandwich

Ingredients

- 2 red peppers
- 150g oven roast beef
- Fresh bocconcini
- Chipotle lime mayonnaise
- Arugula

Directions

a) When shopping, try to choose red peppers that have at least 2 flat sides. The flat sides will work best for the sandwich. If you are lucky, you can find a large pepper that has 3 or 4 sides you can use.

b) Cut the pepper so as to make a nice flat piece that will work as a piece of bread.

c) Now either on the BBQ or in a fry pan, lightly grill the pepper for about 2 minutes on each side. This will soften the pepper up a little.

d) Now using the peppers as your bread, build your sandwich. Spread a little mayo on the pepper and then add the beef.

e) Next put on a few slices of bocconcini, top with a little arugula, add a touch more mayo to the top pepper slice and place on top.

16. Sweet Potato Burger Buns

Ingredients

- 1 Large Sweet Potato
- 2 Teaspoons Olive Oil
- Salt and Pepper

Directions

a) Peel and dice your sweet potatoes into the shapes of burger buns.

b) You need 2 medium slices for each burger you are making. You can cook up to 16 slices at once in the air fryer, before your air fryer becomes overcrowded.

c) Using your hands rub the olive oil over them.

d) Season with salt and pepper.

e) Cook for 10 minutes at 180c/360f in the air fryer.

f) Place your Mediterranean burgers in between two sweet potato burger bun slices and serve.

17.   Tuna Pickle Boats

YIELD: 12 Pickle boats

Ingredients

- 6 whole baby dill pickles or 2 large whole pickles
- 5 oz. chunk white tuna
- $\frac{1}{4}$ cup mayonnaise
- $\frac{1}{4}$ cup diced red onion
- 1 teaspoons sugar or honey

Directions

a) Cut whole pickles in half from end to end, lengthwise. Using a spoon or paring knife, cut or scrape out the inside of each side of the pickle to create a boat shape with the remaining pickle skin.

b) Chop up the scraped out insides and place them in a mixing bowl. Using a paper towel, soak up any extra juices from the pickle boats and chopped inside pieces.

c) Thoroughly drain tuna and add to bowl. Press with a fork to chop up large chunks. Add mayonnaise, red onion, chopped pickle, and sugar or honey (optional) and mix well to form the tuna salad.

d) Spoon tuna salad into each pickle boat. Chill and serve or serve immediately.

18. Grilled Portobello Burgers

Makes 4 burgers

Ingredients

- 2 tablespoons olive oil
- 1 tablespoon balsamic vinegar
- $1/4$ teaspoon sugar
- $1/4$ teaspoon salt
- $1/8$ teaspoon freshly ground black pepper
- 4 large portobello mushroom caps, lightly rinsed and patted dry
- 4 slices red onion
- 4 kaiser rolls, halved horizontally or other burger rolls
- 8 large fresh basil leaves
- 4 slices ripe tomato

Directions

a) Preheat the grill or broiler. In a small bowl, combine the oil, vinegar, sugar, salt, and pepper. Set aside.

b) Place the mushroom caps and onion slices on the hot grill and cook until grilled on both sides, turning once, about 10 minutes' total.

c) Brush the tops of the mushrooms and onion with the vinaigrette and keep warm. Place the rolls cut side down on the grill and lightly toast, about 1 minute.

d) Layer an onion slice and mushroom onto the bottom half of each roll. Top each with two basil leaves and a tomato slice.

Drizzle with any remaining vinaigrette and cover each burger with the roll tops. Serve immediately.

19.   Burgers with tofu

Ingredients

- ½ cup Bulgur
- 2 large Carrots; shredded
- 4 ounces Firm tofu
- 1 Egg white
- 3 tablespoons Chopped fresh mint
- 3 tablespoons Minced scallions
- ¼ teaspoon Cayenne pepper
- ⅓ cup Plain panko; dried
- ⅓ cup Flour; divided use
- 2 tablespoons Light ketchup
- 2 teaspoons Dijon mustard
- 4 Hamburger buns
- 4 Romaine lettuce leaves
- 4 large Tomato slices
- ½ cup Alfalfa sprouts

Directions

a) In a large covered saucepan, bring the water and salt to a boil over medium heat. Add the bulgur and carrots, remove from the heat.

b) In a large bowl, mash the tofu. Stir in the bulgur mixture, egg white, mint, scallions and cayenne, stirring well. Stir in the panko, $\frac{1}{4}$ cup of the flour, the ketchup and mustard.

c) Form the bulgur mixture into patties, fry.

20. Portabella and Halloumi Burgers

Makes two servings

Ingredients

- 4 portabella mushroom caps
- 3 1/2 tablespoons of balsamic vinegar
- 2 tablespoons of olive oil
- 2 slices of tomato
- 2 slices of halloumi
- Handful of basil leaves
- Sea salt
- Freshly ground pepper

Directions

a) Grill the portabella mushrooms. You can either grill or broil the mushrooms. To grill, preheat the grill to 450 °F (232 °C) (232 Celsius). Alternately, you can preheat your oven broiler and put the rack on the top third of the oven. While you are waiting for the oven or grill to heat up, remove the steps of the portabella mushrooms. Brush the mushrooms with the olive oil and sprinkle a bit of sea salt on top of them. Grill or broil them for four or five minutes per side.

b) Grill the halloumi. Slice the halloumi into desirable, relatively thin slices (e.g., half an inch thick). Grill it for two minutes per side on high heat. The halloumi should be soft and emit an aromatic, salty smell.

c) Assemble the sandwich. The portabella mushrooms will be your bun. On top of one Portobello mushroom cap, place the grilled Halloumi cheese, slice of tomato and basil leaves. Add the balsamic vinegar and the freshly ground pepper. Then, place the other mushroom cap on top. Repeat this process for the other burger.

21. Tuna Salad Sandwiches with Cucumber

Makes 4 sandwiches

Ingredients

- 2 long, English cucumbers
- 1 tablespoon of red wine vinegar
- 1/4 of plain yogurt
- 1/4 of chopped dill
- 1/4 of celery leaves
- 1 tablespoon of extra-virgin olive oil
- Kosher salt
- Freshly ground black pepper
- 2 sliced scallions
- 2 tablespoons of mayonnaise
- 1 stalk of sliced celery stalk
- 1/2 teaspoon of lemon zest
- 2 five ounce cans of light tuna, drained
- 1/2 cup of alfalfa sprouts

Directions

a) Prepare the cucumbers. You have two options for preparing the cucumbers, which will be used instead of the bread for this tuna sandwich. If you are making appetizer sandwiches, you should simply peel and then slice the cucumber horizontally, into quarter inch slices. This option will give you a greater number of smaller tuna sandwiches. Alternately, if you want to make a sub style tuna sandwich, you can halve the cucumbers lengthwise. Then, scoop out the seeds and flesh to make little boats, where you will put the tuna mix. Poke the inside a bit with a fork, so that the cucumber absorbs more of the flavor.

b) Mix the vinaigrette. In a medium-sized bowl, whisk the mustard, vinegar, salt and black pepper. Then, slowly whisk in the olive oil. Finally, pour the vinaigrette onto the cucumber.

c) Make the tuna filling. Start by draining the tuna fish. Rinse it well with cold water, and then put it aside. In a small bowl, whisk the mayonnaise, yogurt, dill, celery leaves, scallions, celery, lemon zest, quarter teaspoon of salt and a pinch of black pepper. Throw the tuna into the bowl and then mix to combine all ingredients.

d) Put together the sandwiches. If you are making the appetizer version, place a dollop of tuna mix and then a few sprouts on top of each slice of cucumber. Then, add another slice on top for a cute little sandwich. If you are making the sub style tuna sandwich, fill the cucumber boats with the tuna mixture and then add the sprouts. Add the other half of the cucumber on top. Eat and enjoy!

22.   Mediterranean Wrap with Tofu or Chicken

Ingredients

- 1 large leaf of butter lettuce
- 2 tablespoons of hummus
- 1/2 cup of bean sprouts
- 2 ounces (i.e., half a cup) of diced tofu or chopped, cooked chicken breast
- 1 teaspoon of za'atar or sesame seeds

Directions

a) Prepare the lettuce. Place the leaf of lettuce so that the rib is horizontal. If you do not have a big enough leaf, you can always glue two pieces of butter lettuce together with some hummus. Simply place a thin layer of hummus on the edge of one piece of lettuce and then place the second piece of lettuce over top and press down.

b) Spread the hummus. Start by evenly spreading the hummus over the bottom third of the lettuce leaf. You want to spread it in an even layer, rather than just a big dollop. You should have a two-inch border around the leaf.

c) Assemble the wrap. Place the tofu or cooked, sliced chicken breast in the middle of the wrap. Then, add the sprouts. Evenly distribute the za-atar over top all of the ingredients. Then, roll up your wrap. Start by folding in the sides to the center. Then, roll it up horizontally, rolling it up away from you as if you were making a burrito. You can either enjoy it right away or wrap it in plastic wrap and refrigerate it. It will be good for twenty four hours.

23.   Ham and Cheese Sandwich

Serves four people

Ingredients

- 1 medium jicama, four inches long
- 1 tablespoon of sour cream
- 1 tablespoon of sliced chives
- 1 teaspoon of Dijon mustard
- 1 teaspoon of horseradish
- 6 ounces of deli ham
- 4 slices of Havarti cheese
- 2 cups of baby arugula
- Dill pickle spears, optional
- Freshly ground black pepper
- Salt to taste
- 4 chard leaves
- 1 avocado
- 1/2 a red bell pepper, sliced
- 1 grated carrot
- 1 sliced tomato

- 1 scallion, chopped into four
- 1 sliced cucumber
- 1/2 a beet
- 1 cup of basil leaves
- 1/2 a cup of walnuts
- 1 garlic clove
- 2tablespoons of lemon juice
- 1/4 cup of olive oil
- Salt and pepper to taste

Directions

a) Peel and slice the jicama. Using a vegetable peeler or a sharp knife, peel the jicama. Like you are peeling a potato, make sure you get off all of the skin. Then, slice the jicama into thin, approximately one eight inch slices.

b) Mix the sauce. In a small bowl, stir the sour cream, mustard, horseradish, chives, and a pinch of freshly ground black pepper. Add salt to taste.

c) Assemble the ham and cheese sandwiches. Start by laying out the slices of jicama. On each slice, spread a layer of sauce. Then, add a quarter of the ham, cheese and arugula to each of the four sandwiches. Top each sandwich with a jicama slice. Cut each sandwich in half and serve with a pickle on the side.

24.   Swiss Chard Wrap with Pesto

4 chard leaves

Ingredients

- 1 avocado
- 1/2 a red bell pepper, sliced
- 1 grated carrot
- 1 sliced tomato
- 1 scallion, chopped into four
- 1 sliced cucumber
- 1/2 a beet
- 1 cup of basil leaves
- 1/2 a cup of walnuts
- 1 garlic clove
- 1 or two tablespoons of lemon juice
- 1/4 cup of olive oil
- Salt and pepper to taste

Directions

a) Prepare the Swiss chard leaves. Wash the Swiss chard leaves and pat them dry. Then, cut off the stem. You will need to cut it off a little bit into the actual leaf as well, approximately half an inch up from the bottom of the leaf.

b) Blend the pesto. In a small food processor, throw in all of the pesto ingredients. This should include the basil, walnuts, olive oil, lemon juice, garlic, salt and pepper to taste. Mix it all together until you get a nice smooth pesto.

c) Assemble the wraps. Add a couple tablespoons of pesto to each Swiss chard leaf. Then, throw in the rest of the ingredients. Fold in the sides of the Swiss chard leaf. Finally, roll it up like a burrito. Roll it away from your body. Enjoy it right away or wrap it with plastic wrap and put it in the fridge.

BURGERS

25. Chicken Sushi Burger

Servings: 2

Ingredients

Sushi Rice

- 1 cup of sushi rice 8oz., washed till the water runs clear, and then left in the strainer for a few minutes.
- 1 cup of cold water
- ¼ cup black sesame seeds optional
- Sushi Seasoning
- ¼ cup mirin
- ¼ cup rice wine vinegar
- ¼ cup white sugar
- 1 Tablespoons salt use less if using seasoned rice wine vinegar

Chicken

- 1 chicken breast will make 2 cutlets, OR 2 thigh pieces
- 1 egg
- Splash of milk
- Salt
- Panko Crumbs
- Oil for shallow frying

- Chicken Marinade
- 1 Tablespoons Soy Sauce
- 1 Tablespoons Rice wine vinegar
- 1 teaspoons garlic powder
- 1/2 teaspoons cayenne pepper reduce if you like it less spicy
- 1 Tablespoons brown sugar

Spicy Tomato Sauce

- ½ cup ketchup sauce
- 2 Tablespoons mirin
- 1 teaspoons crushed chili flakes
- 1 Tablespoons Worcestershire sauce
- Splash of water
- Asian Spring Onion Omelet
- 2 eggs
- 2 Tablespoons milk
- Generous splash of fish sauce or soy sauce
- 3 spring onions sliced thin

To Serve

- Kewpie

- Mayonnaise
- Furikake Seasoning

Directions

Sushi Rice Buns

a) Place all the ingredients in a small saucepan and heat on medium heat. Stir to make sure the sugar and salt dissolve. Once it comes to a light boil, remove from the heat and set aside.

b) Let the washed rice dry in a colander or sieve for about 5 - 10 minutes. Place the rice and the water in a rice cooker and let it cook according to the manufacturer's instructions. Keep the rice warm until ready to use.

c) When you're ready to make the sushi burgers, spread the rice in a larger bowl or container.

d) Sprinkle $\frac{1}{4}$ cup of black sesame seeds on top. Keep a wet cloth handy.

e) Measure out roughly a 1/4 cup of the sushi seasoning and sprinkle on top of the rice, and using a wide spoon (like a rice paddle) "chop" and fold the rice lightly, taking care not to squash or break the rice.

f) Roughly divide the rice into 4 equal portions.

g) Shaping sushi "buns" by hand - with wet hands, shape each portion into a burger bun. Keep them on a plate covered with the wet cloth.

h) Shaping sushi "buns" with an egg ring - place wet egg rings on a parchment paper and place one portion of rice in the egg ring. Using a wet spoon, press the rice into the egg rings until it forms a compact, molded rice "bun".

i) In a small nonstick frying pan, brush some oil and sear just one side of each rice bun for about 3 - 5 minutes on medium heat, or until it starts to caramelize a little. Set aside and keep covered with a wet cloth.

Chicken

j) Butterfly the chicken breast and cut it into half so you have 2 thin (1cm thin) chicken breast fillets. Or you can use a meat hammer to pound chicken thighs into thin fillets.

k) Add the marinade ingredients into a bowl and add the chicken fillets and let them marinate for a few hours (optional).

l) In a bowl, place the eggs, cream, salt and whisk to combine. Dunk the chicken in the egg wash and coat completely. Then coat with the panko panko crumbs. Set aside until ready to be fried.

m) Heat oil in a pan on medium high heat to shallow fry the chicken cutlets. When the oil is heated (about 350°F), carefully place the breaded chicken cutlet (do not over crowd the pan) and fry it 4 minutes on each side until golden brown and cooked through (mine took 4 minutes on each side). Set it on a draining rack to drain the oil. You can keep it warm in the oven until needed.

Spicy Ketchup Sauce

n) Place all the ingredients in a small pan. Under medium heat, bring the ingredients to a simmer while mixing. Set aside to cool. If it's too thick, add a splash of water.

o) Asian Spring Onion Omelet

p) Whisk the eggs, cream and fish sauce in a bowl.

q) Place two egg rings in a non-stick pan and heat on medium heat. Spray the egg rings with some oil spray to prevent the eggs from sticking.

r) Divide the egg mix between the two rings. Add spring onions to the top of the omelet and let it cook until the eggs are set.

s) If you don't have egg rings, make 1 omelet at a time in a small pan, sprinkle spring onions and fold it once to make smaller omelets to fit the burger.

Assembling Sushi Burgers

t) Slice the breaded chicken cutlets.

u) Brush the sushi rice bun with the spicy ketchup sauce (Tonkatsu sauce). Place the sliced chicken on the rice bun.

Spoon some spicy ketchup sauce (or Tonkatsu sauce) on top of the chicken.

v) Place the omelet on top of that, followed by the kewpie or mayonnaise. Top with a second sushi rice bun. Enjoy!

26. Tomato Avocado Burgers

Servings 4

Ingredients

- 4 large tomatoes
- 1-pound grass fed organic ground beef
- 1/4 teaspoon ground black pepper
- 1/2 plus 1/4 teaspoons fine grain sea salt
- 1 teaspoon chili powder
- 1 ripe avocado, divided
- 2 tablespoons Greek yogurt
- 1 tablespoon mayonnaise
- 2 teaspoons fresh lime juice
- 1/4 teaspoon ground cumin
- Handful alfalfa sprouts

Directions

a) Place half of the avocado in a bowl and mash with a fork until almost smooth. Add yogurt, mayo, lime juice and cumin and stir to combine. Dice remaining half of the avocado and add it alongside $\frac{1}{4}$ teaspoon salt. Stir gently to combine. Set aside.

b) In a bowl season ground beef with ½ teaspoon of salt, black pepper and chili powder and mix well.

c) Preheat grill (or grill pan) to medium-high heat. Grill patties 3 minutes on each side or until desired degree of doneness.

d) In the meantime, lightly grease with olive oil a medium non-stick pan/skillet and heat over medium-high heat. Cook halved tomatoes face down for 2 to 3 minutes, until they begin to brown.

e) To assemble burgers, place a large pinch of sprouts on the bottom part of each tomato, top with a beef patty, about 2 tablespoons of avocado sauce and finish with the other half of each tomato.

27. Red Beet Burgers with Arugula

Ingredients

SERVES 4

- 15 oz. Light Red Kidney Beans (can)
- 2 1/2 Tablespoons extra-virgin olive oil
- 2 1/2 oz. Cremini Mushroom
- 1 medium red onion
- 1/2 cup cooked brown rice
- 3/4 cup Beets Raw
- 1/3 cup Hemp Seeds
- 1 teaspoons ground black pepper
- 1/2 teaspoons sea salt
- 1/2 teaspoons Ground Coriander Seed
- 1/2 teaspoons Worcestershire Sauce
- 1 egg(s)
- 4 cups Organic Baby Arugula
- 2 teaspoons White Balsamic Vinegar
- 1/3 cup Goat Cheese Crumbles

Directions

a) Preheat the oven to 375°F. Mash the kidney beans well in a large mixing bowl; set aside.

b) Heat 1 tablespoon of the oil in a large nonstick skillet over medium. Add the mushrooms and three-quarters of the onion and sauté until softened, about 8 minutes.

c) Transfer the vegetable mixture to the large mixing bowl with the beans. Stir in the rice, beets, hemp seeds, pepper, salt, coriander, and Worcestershire sauce until combined. Add the egg (or vegan egg replacer) and stir until well combined.

d) Form the mixture into four balls; place onto a large unbleached parchment paper-lined baking sheet. Pat with your fingertips into four (4-inch-diameter) patties. Lightly dab the top of the patties with 1/2 tablespoon of the oil using your fingertips. Bake for 1 hour. Very gently flip over each burger and bake until crisped, firm, and browned, about 20 minutes more. Let stand for at least 5 minutes to complete the cooking process.

e) Toss the arugula with the vinegar and remaining 1 tablespoon oil, arrange on top of each burger. Sprinkle with the remaining onion and goat cheese, and serve.

28. Macadamia-Cashew Patties

Makes 4 patties

Ingredients

- 1 cup chopped macadamia nuts
- 1 cup chopped cashews
- 1 medium carrot, grated
- 1 small onion, chopped
- 1 garlic clove, mince
- 1 jalapeño or other green chile, seeded and minced
- 1 cup old-fashioned oats
- 1 cup dry unseasoned panko
- 2 tablespoons minced fresh cilantro
- 1/2 teaspoon ground coriander
- Salt and freshly ground black pepper
- 2 teaspoons fresh lime juice
- Canola or grapeseed oil, for frying
- 4 sandwich rolls
- Lettuce leaves and condiment of choice

Directions

a) In a food processor, combine the macadamia nuts, cashews, carrot, onion, garlic, chile, oats, panko, cilantro, coriander, and salt and pepper to taste. Process until well mixed. Add the lime juice and process until well blended. Taste, adjusting seasonings if necessary. Shape the mixture into 4 equal patties.

b) In a large skillet, heat a thin layer of oil over medium heat. Add the patties and cook until golden brown on both sides, turning once, about 10 minutes total. Serve on sandwich rolls with lettuce and condiments of choice.

29. Pecan-Lentil Burgers

Makes 4 to 6 burgers

Ingredients

- 1 1/2 cups cooked brown lentil
- 1/2 cup ground pecans
- 1/2 cup old-fashioned oats
- 1/4 cup dry unseasoned panko
- 1/4 cup wheat gluten flour (vital wheat gluten)
- 1/2 cup minced onion
- 1/4 cup minced fresh parsley
- 1 teaspoon Dijon mustard
- 1/2 teaspoon salt
- 1/8 teaspoon freshly ground pepper
- 2 tablespoons olive oi
- 4 to 6 burger rolls
- Lettuce leaves, sliced tomato, sliced red onion, and condiments of choice

Directions

a) In a food processor, combine the lentils, pecans, oats, panko, flour, onion, parsley, mustard, salt, and pepper. Pulse to combine, leaving some texture. Shape the lentil mixture into 4 to 6 burgers.

b) In a large skillet, heat the oil over medium heat. Add the burgers and cook until golden brown, about 5 minutes per side.

c) Serve the burgers on the rolls with lettuce, tomato slices, onion, and condiments of choice.

30.   Black Bean Burgers

Makes 4 burgers

Ingredients

- 3 tablespoons olive oil
- 1/2 cup minced onion
- 1 garlic clove, minced
- 1 1/2 cups cooked or 1 (15.5-ounce) can black beans, drained and rinsed
- 1 tablespoon minced fresh parsley
- 1/2 cup dry unseasoned panko
- 1/4 cup wheat gluten flour (vital wheat gluten)
- 1 teaspoon smoked paprika
- 1/2 teaspoon dried thyme
- Salt and freshly ground black pepper
- 4 burger rolls
- 4 lettuce leaves
- 1 ripe tomato, cut into 1/4-inch slices

Directions

a) In a small skillet, heat 1 tablespoon of the oil over medium heat. Add the onion and garlic and cook until softened, about 5 minutes.

b) Transfer the onion mixture to a food processor. Add the beans, parsley, panko, flour, paprika, thyme, and salt and pepper to taste. Process until well combined, leaving some texture. Shape the mixture into 4 equal patties and refrigerate for 20 minutes.

c) In a large skillet, heat the remaining 2 tablespoons oil over medium heat. Add the burgers and cook until browned on both sides, turning once, about 5 minutes per side.

d) Serve the burgers on the rolls with lettuce and tomato slices.

31. Some-Kind of-Nut Burgers

Makes 4 burgers

Ingredients

- 2 tablespoons plus 1 teaspoon olive oil
- 1 small onion, chopped
- 1 medium carrot, grated
- 1 cup unsalted mixed nut
- 1/4 cup wheat gluten flour (vital wheat gluten), plus more if needed
- 1/2 cup old-fashioned oats, plus more if needed
- 2 tablespoons creamy peanut butter
- 2 tablespoons minced fresh parsley
- 1/2 teaspoon salt
- 1/4 teaspoon freshly ground black pepper
- 4 burger rolls
- 4 lettuce leaves
- 1 ripe tomato, cut into 1/4-inch slices

Directions

a) In a medium skillet, heat 1 teaspoon of the oil over medium heat. Add the onion and cook until soft, about 5 minutes. Stir in the carrot and set aside.

b) In a food processor, pulse the nuts until chopped. Add the onion-carrot mixture along with the flour, oats, peanut butter, parsley, salt, and pepper. Process until well blended. Shape the mixture into 4 equal patties, about 4 inches in diameter. If the mixture is too loose, add a little more flour or oats.

c) In a large skillet, heat the remaining 2 tablespoons oil over medium heat, add the burgers and cook until browned on both sides, about 5 minutes per side.

d) Serve the burgers on the rolls with lettuce and tomato slices.

32. Golden Veggie Burgers

Makes 4 burgers

Ingredients

- 2 tablespoons olive oil
- 1 small yellow onion, chopped
- 1/2 small yellow bell pepper, chopped
- 1 1/2 cups cooked or 1 (15.5-ounce) can chickpeas, drained and rinsed
- 3/4 teaspoon salt
- 1/4 teaspoon freshly ground black pepper
- 1/4 cup wheat gluten flour (vital wheat gluten)
- 4 burger rolls
- Condiments of choice

Directions

a) In a large skillet, heat 1 tablespoon of the oil over medium heat. Add the onion and pepper and cook until softened, about 5 minutes. Set aside to cool slightly.

b) Transfer the cooled onion mixture to a food processor. Add the chickpeas, salt, and black pepper and pulse to mix. Add the flour and process to combine.

c) Shape the mixture into 4 burgers, about 4 inches in diameter. If the mixture is too loose, add a little extra flour.

d) In a large skillet, heat the remaining 2 tablespoons of oil over medium heat. Add the burgers and cook until firm and browned on both sides, turning once, about 5 minutes per side.

e) Serve the burgers on the rolls with condiments of choice.

33. White Bean and Walnut Patties

Makes 4 patties

Ingredients

- 1/4 cup diced onion
- 1 garlic clove, crushed
- 1 cup walnut pieces
- 1 cup canned or cooked white beans, drained and rinsed
- 1 cup wheat gluten flour (vital wheat gluten)
- 2 tablespoons minced fresh parsley
- 1 tablespoon soy sauce
- 1 teaspoon Dijon mustard, plus more to serve
- 1/2 teaspoon salt
- 1/2 teaspoon ground sage
- 1/2 teaspoon sweet paprika
- 1/4 teaspoon turmeric
- 1/4 teaspoon freshly ground black pepper
- 2 tablespoons olive oil
- Lettuce leaves and sliced tomatoes

Directions

a) In a food processor, combine the onion, garlic, and walnuts and process until finely ground.

b) Cook the beans in a small skillet over medium heat, stirring, for 1 to 2 minutes to evaporate any moisture. Add the beans to the food processor along with the flour, parsley, soy sauce, mustard, salt, sage, paprika, turmeric, and pepper. Process until well blended. Shape the mixture into 4 equal patties.

c) In a large skillet, heat the oil over medium heat. Add the patties and cook until browned on both sides, about 5 minutes per side.

d) Serve with lettuce, and sliced tomatoes.

34.   Curried Chickpea Patties

Makes 4 patties

Ingredients

- 3 tablespoons olive oil
- 1 small onion, chopped
- 1 1/2 teaspoons hot or mild curry powder
- 1/2 teaspoon salt
- 1/8 teaspoon ground cayenne
- 1 cup cooked chickpeas
- 1 tablespoon chopped fresh parsley
- 1/2 cup wheat gluten flour
- 1/3 cup dry unseasoned panko
- 1/4 cup vegan mayonnaise
- Lettuce leaves
- 1 ripe tomato, cut into 1/4-inch slices

Directions

a) In a large skillet, heat 1 tablespoon of the oil over medium heat. Add the onion, cover, and cook until softened, 5 minutes. Stir in 1 teaspoon of the curry powder, salt, and cayenne and remove from the heat. Set aside.

b) In a food processor, combine the chickpeas, parsley, wheat gluten flour, panko, and the cooked onion. Process to combine, leaving some texture.

c) Form the chickpea mixture into 4 equal patties and set aside.

d) In a large skillet, heat the remaining 2 tablespoons oil over medium heat. Add the patties, cover, and cook until golden brown on both sides, turning once, about 5 minutes per side.

e) In a small bowl, combine the remaining 1/2 teaspoon of curry powder with the mayonnaise, stirring to blend.

35. Pinto Bean Patties with Mayo

Makes 4 patties

Ingredients

- 1 1/2 cups cooked or 1 (15.5-ounce) can pinto beans, rinsed and drained
- 1 medium shallot, chopped
- 1 garlic clove, mince
- 2 tablespoons chopped fresh cilantro
- 1 teaspoon Creole seasoning
- 1/4 cup wheat gluten flour
- Salt and freshly ground black pepper
- 1/2 cup dry unseasoned panko
- 1 cup vegan mayonnaise
- 2 teaspoons fresh lime juice
- 1 serrano chile, seeded and minced
- 2 tablespoons olive oil
- Shredded lettuce
- 1 tomato, cut into 1/4-inch slices

Directions

a) Blot the beans with paper towels to absorb excess moisture. In a food processor, combine the beans, shallot, garlic, cilantro, Creole seasoning, flour, and salt and pepper to taste. Process until well blended.

b) Shape the mixture into 4 equal patties, adding more flour if needed. Dredge the patties in the panko. Refrigerate for 20 minutes.

c) In a small bowl, combine the mayonnaise, lime juice, and serrano chile. Season with the salt and pepper to taste, mix well, and refrigerate until ready to serve.

d) In a large skillet, heat the oil over medium heat. Add the patties and cook until browned and crispy on both sides, about 5 minutes per side.

e) Serve the patties, lettuce, and tomato.

36. Vegan Veggie burger

Yield: 1 Serving

Ingredient

- 1 Hamburger Buns, Low Calorie
- 1 Hamburger Patty
- 1-ounce Red Onion -- sliced
- $\frac{1}{2}$ ounce Roma Tomato -- sliced
- $\frac{3}{4}$ ounce Romaine Lettuce
- $1\frac{1}{2}$ teaspoon Ketchup
- $1\frac{1}{2}$ teaspoon Vegan Nonfat Mayonnaise
- $1\frac{1}{2}$ tablespoon Vegan Bacon Pieces

Directions

a) Put hamburger patty and onion on GRILL EXPRESS.

b) Grill for 1 to $1\frac{1}{2}$ minutes. Pile on bun spread with vegan mayonnaise, ketchup. Add lettuce and sprinkle bacon pieces over all.

37. Garbanzo bean burgers

Yield: 6 servings

Ingredient

- 2 cups Mashed garbanzo beans
- 1 each Stalk celery, finely chopped
- 1 each Carrot, finely chopped
- ¼ small Onion, minced
- ¼ cup Whole wheat flour
- Salt and pepper to taste
- 2 teaspoons Oil

Directions

a) Mix the ingredients (except oil) in a bowl. Form 6 flat patties.

b) Fry in oiled pan over medium-high heat until burgers are golden brown on each side.

38. Bulgur patties

Yield: 4 servings

Ingredients

- 1 clove garlic, minced
- ¼ cup bulgur wheat
- 1 can chickpeas, drained (19 oz.)
- ¼ cup sesame seeds, toasted
- 1 onion
- 1 Teaspoon lemon juice
- ½ Teaspoon salt
- ¼ Teaspoon pepper
- 4 carrots, grated
- 1 rib celery, chopped

Directions

a) In saucepan, bring water to boiling. Add bulgur; cover and simmer 8 minutes. In food processor puree chickpeas, sesame seeds, onion, lemon juice, salt, pepper and garlic until smooth.

b) In bowl combine chickpea mixture, cooked bulgur, carrots and celery. Form burgers. Lightly oil rack set in broiler pan. Place burgers on rack.

c) Preheat broiler. Broil 18 minutes, 3" from heat, turning once.

39. All-star veggie patty

Yield: 1 Serving

Ingredient

- 8 ounces Rolled oats
- 4 ounces Vegan mozzarella cheese
- 3 ounces Shiitake mushrooms diced
- 3 ounces Egg whites
- 3 ounces' White onion diced
- 2 Garlic cloves minced
- 2 ounces Red pepper diced
- 2 ounces Zucchini dice

Directions

a) Combine all ingredients in a food processor. Pulse the on/off switch to roughly combine ingredients

b) Do not over mix. Final mixing can be done by hand. Form into four ounce patties.

c) In a skillet add a small amount of olive oil. When pan is hot, add patty. Cook one minute per side.

40.   Oatmeal veggie patty

Ingredient

- ½ cup Green onion -- chopped
- ¼ cup Green pepper -- chopped
- ¼ cup Parsley -- chopped
- ¼ teaspoon White pepper
- 2 Garlic cloves -- diced
- ½ cup Vegan Mozzarella cheese -- grated
- ¾ cup Brown rice
- ⅓ cup; water -- white wine
- ½ cup Carrot -- shredded
- ⅔ cup Onion -- chopped
- 3 Celery stalks -- chopped
- 1¼ teaspoon Seasoning salt
- ¾ teaspoon Thyme
- ½ cup Vegan Cheddar cheese -- grated
- 2 cups Oatmeal -- quick
- ¾ cup Bulgur wheat

Directions

a) Cook the rice and bulgur wheat. Braise vegetables for -2-3 minutes in a covered pan, stirring once or twice. Veggies should still be crisp. Drain thoroughly; mix with rice and cheese until cheese melts slightly.

b) Mix in remaining ingredients. Shape in 4-ounce patties. Cook about 10 minutes each on a grill or nonstick frying pan, using cooking spray. Serve on a whole wheat bun.

41.   Bulgur Lentil veggie patty

Yield: 6 servings

Ingredient

- 2 cups Cooked lentils
- 1 cup Smoked Portobello mushrooms,
- 1 cup Bulgur wheat
- 2 Cloves roasted garlic,
- 1 tablespoon Worcestershire
- 2 tablespoons Walnut oil
- ¼ teaspoon Tarragon, minced
- Salt and pepper to taste

Directions

a) Prepare a wood or charcoal grill and let it burn down to embers.

b) In a large mixing bowl, mash lentils until smooth. Add all other ingredients and mix until thoroughly combined. Refrigerate for at least 2 hours. Form into burgers. Brush the burgers with olive oil and grill for 6 minutes on each side or until done. Serve hot with your favorite condiments.

42. Veggie patties

Ingredient

- ½ cup Uncooked bulgur
- ½ cup Boiling water
- 1 cup Diced baking potato
- 3 cups Water
- 1 cup Finely diced zucchini
- ½ cup Chopped onion
- ¼ cup Chopped fresh parsley
- 2 Garlic cloves; minced
- 5 Hamburger buns
- ½ cup Nonfat sour cream
- ¼ cup Diced seeded peeled cucumber
- ¼ teaspoon Dried dill
- 1 Garlic clove; minced
- ½ cup Crumbled Vegan feta cheese
- 5 Tomato slices; 1/4-inch thick

Directions

a) BURGERS: Combine bulgur and boiling water in a large bowl. Cover and let stand 30 minutes. Meanwhile, combine potato and 3 cups water in a saucepan; bring to a boil.

b) Reduce heat; simmer until tender, 5 to 10 minutes, and drain. Cool.

c) Stir together bulgur, potato, zucchini, onion, parsley, garlic, salt, and pepper in a large bowl. Divide mixture into 5 equal portions and shape into $\frac{1}{2}$-inch-thick patties.

d) Place a large nonstick skillet coated with cooking spray over medium-high heat until hot. Cook patties 4 minutes on each side.

43.   Mushroom tofu patty

Ingredient

- ½ cup Rolled oats
- 1¼ cup Coarsely chopped almonds
- 1 tablespoon Olive or canola oil
- ½ cup Chopped green onion
- 2 teaspoons Minced garlic
- 1½ cup Chopped Cremini
- ½ cup Cooked rice; brown basmati
- ⅓ cup Vegan cheddar cheese
- ⅔ cup Mashed firm tofu
- 1 large Egg; plus
- 1 Egg white; lightly beaten
- 3 tablespoons Chopped parsley
- ½ cup Dry panko
- 6 slices Fresh mozzarella; if desired

Directions

a) Heat oil in a sauté pan and over moderate heat sauté the onions, garlic and mushrooms until softened and lightly colored. Add the oats and continue to cook for another 2 minutes, stirring constantly.

b) Combine the onion mixture with the rice, cheese, tofu, eggs. Parsley, panko and almonds and stir to combine. Season to taste with salt and pepper. Shape into 6 patties and sauté or broil until golden and crisp on the outside.

c) Top with a slice of fresh mozzarella and a teaspoon or two of fresh salsa and serve immediately as is.

44. Ovo veggie patty

Yield: 1 servings

Ingredient

- ½ Chopped Onion
- ½ cup Cooked Green lentils
- ⅓ cup Cooked peas
- 1 Grated Carrot
- 1 tablespoon Chopped Fresh Parsley
- 1 teaspoon Tamari
- 2 cups panko
- ¼ cup Flour
- 1 Beaten Egg

Directions

a) Sauté the onion until soft Mix all ingredients except the flour and leave to cool Form the mixture into patties and brown in skillet.

b) Green Lentils take about one hour to cook from dry, but they freeze well, so make a big bunch of them at once.

45. Quick veggie patties

Yield: 4 servings

Ingredient

- 10 ounces Vegetables, mixed, frozen
- 1 Egg white
- pinch Salt and pepper
- ½ cup Mushrooms, fresh; chopped
- ½ cup panko
- 1 medium Onion; sliced

Directions

a) Preheat oven to 350 degrees.
b) Steam vegetables until just tender
c) Set aside to cool.
d) Fine chop steamed vegetables and mix with egg white, salt, pepper, mushrooms and panko.
e) Form mixture into patties.
f) Place patties, topped with onion slices, on a lightly oiled baking sheet and bake, turning once, until brown and crispy on both sides, about 45 minutes.

46. TexMex veggie patty

Ingredient

- 15¼ ounce Canned whole kernel corn
- ½ cup Liquid reserved
- ½ cup Cornmeal
- ½ cup Onion; finely chopped
- ⅓ cup Red bell pepper; finely chopped
- ½ teaspoon Lime zest; grated
- ¼ cup Cooked white rice
- 3 tablespoons Fresh cilantro; chopped
- 4 teaspoons Jalapeno chile pepper
- ½ teaspoon Ground cumin
- 4 Nonfat flour tortillas; 9- to 10-inch
- 8 tablespoons Light sour cream
- 8 tablespoons Purchased salsa

Directions

a) Blend ½ cup corn kernels and 1 tablespoon cornmeal in processor until moist clumps form. Add ¾ cup corn kernels; process 10 seconds

b) Transfer corn mixture to heavy medium nonstick saucepan. Add ½ cup corn liquid, onion, bell pepper and lime peel. Cover and cook over very low heat until thick and firm, stirring often, 12 minutes. Mix in rice, cilantro, jalapeño, salt and cumin. Drop $\frac{1}{4}$ of mixture onto each of 4 pieces of foil; press pieces into $\frac{3}{4}$-inch-thick patties.

c) Prepare barbecue. Spray both sides of burgers with nonstick spray; grill until crisp, about 5 minutes per side. Grill tortillas until pliable, about 30 seconds per side

47. Veggie bean patties

Yield: 4 servings

Ingredient

- 2 ounces Cooked mixed beans
- 1 small Onion; finely chopped
- 1 Carrot; finely grated
- 1 teaspoon vegetable extract
- 1 teaspoon Dried mixed herbs
- 1-ounce Whole meal panko

Directions

a) Mix all ingredients in a food processor or blender until almost smooth.

b) Shape into 4 thick burgers and chill well.

c) Brush with oil and grill or barbecue for about 15 minutes, turning once or twice.

d) Serve in sesame baps with relish, salad and huge chunky fries!

oat burgers

Yield: 1 Servings

Ingredient

- 4 cups Water
- ½ cup Salt-reduced soy sauce
- ½ cup Nutritional yeast
- 1 large Onion diced
- ½ tablespoon Garlic powder
- 1 tablespoon Each Oregano and Basil
- 4½ cup Old fashioned rolled oats

Directions

a) Bring all ingredients except the oats to a boil. Turn heat to low and stir in 4½ cups rolled oats. Cook for about 5 minutes until the water is absorbed.

b) Fill a rectangular non-stick baking pan with the mixture

c) Bake at 350 F. for 25 minutes. Then use a utensil that won't scratch your pan to cut the giant burger into 3½" to 4" (10 cm.) square burgers and flip them over. Cook another 20 minutes.

d) Serve in buns or as a main course, hot or cold. Can be frozen

49.   Walnut and veggie patties

Ingredient

- ½ Red onion
- 1 Rib celery
- 1 Carrot
- ½ Red bell pepper
- 1 cup Walnuts, toasted, ground
- ½ cup panko
- ½ cup orzo pasta
- 2 Eggs
- Salt and pepper
- Buns
- Avocado slices
- Vegan Swiss cheese slices
- Red onion slices
- Catsup
- Mustard

Directions

a) Sauté onion celery, carrots and red bell pepper in 1t oil until soft

b) Cover if desired. Garlic may be added if desired. Add nuts, crumbs, and rice. Form into patties. Fry in 1t oil until golden. Place on bun and assemble.

50. Wild mushroom patty

Ingredient

- 2 teaspoons Olive oil
- 1 medium Yellow onion; chopped fine
- 2 Shallots; peeled and minced
- ⅛ teaspoon Salt
- 1 cup Dry shiitake mushrooms
- 2 cups Portobello mushrooms
- 1 pack Tofu
- ⅓ cup Toasted wheat germ
- ⅓ cup panko
- 2 tablespoons Lite soy sauce
- 2 tablespoons Worcestershire sauce
- 1 teaspoon Liquid smoke flavoring
- ½ teaspoon Granulated garlic
- ¾ cup Quick cooking oats

Directions

a) Sauté onions, shallots, and salt in olive oil for about 5 minutes. Stem softened shiitake mushrooms; mince with fresh mushrooms in a food processor. Add to onions. Cook 10 minutes, stirring occasionally to prevent sticking.

b) Mix mushrooms with mashed tofu, add remaining ingredients and mix well. Wet hands to prevent sticking and form into patties.

c) Bake for 25 minutes, turning once after 15 minutes.

51.   Wonderful veggie patties

Yield: 4 Servings

Ingredient

- 1-pound firm tofu; drained
- 1½ cup Raw oatmeal
- ½ cup Grated carrots
- 1 Chopped sautéed onion
- 1 tablespoon Tahini; more or less
- 2 tablespoons Worcestershire sauce
- 1 tablespoon Soy sauce

Directions

a) Add a mix of whatever spices/herbs you prefer Shape into patties on baking sheets. Bake at 350 for 20 minutes, turn them over and bake for 10 more minutes.

b) They are great hot or cold. We add flavorings to make the spicy.

52. Lentil rice patties

Yield: 8 servings

Ingredient

- ¾ cup Lentils
- 1 Sweet potato
- 10 Fresh spinach leaves; to 15
- 1 cup Fresh mushrooms
- ¾ cup panko
- 1 teaspoon Tarragon
- 1 teaspoon Garlic powder
- 1 teaspoon Parsley flakes
- ¾ cup Long grain rice

Directions

a) A very easy and tasty vegetarian burger taken from Vegetarian Times Mag Aug 93 issue with a few of my own additions.

b) Cook rice till cooked and slightly sticky and lentils till soft. Cool slightly. Finely mince a medium sweet potato which has been peeled and cook until soft. Cool slightly.

c) Finely chop the mushrooms. Spinach leaves should be rinsed and finely shredded. Mix all ingredients and spices together adding salt and pepper to taste.

d) Chill in the refrigerator 15-30 min. Form into patties and sauté in pan or can be done on a vegetable grill on an outdoor grill.

53. Bean and corn patties

Ingredient

- 1 cup Water
- 1½ cup All-purpose flour
- 1 teaspoon Salt
- 2 tablespoons Olive oil
- 3 tablespoons Sugar
- 2 teaspoons Red Star Yeast
- 2 cups Cooked black beans; drained
- 2 cups Corn kernels; drained
- 2 cups Cooked brown rice
- ½ each Large bell pepper; chopped
- 2 teaspoons Ground cumin
- 1 teaspoon Chili powder
- 1 teaspoon Salt; optional
- ½ cup Salsa or picante sauce

Directions

a) Place dough ingredients in pan and select Dough setting and start.

b) Meanwhile, in a large bowl, combine filling ingredients.

c) Gently roll or stretch dough into a 12-inch rope. Divide with a sharp knife, divide the dough into 12 pieces. With a rolling pin, roll each piece into a 6-inch circle. Place $\frac{1}{2}$ cup filling mixture in the center of each circle. Pull the edges up to meet in the center and pinch dough together well to seal.

d) Bake for 15 to 20 minutes until brown. Remove from oven.

54. Black Bean Grillers

Ingredient

- 1 cup (100 g) TVP granules
- 1 cup (235 ml) water
- 1 tablespoon (15 ml) soy sauce
- 1 can (15 ounces, or 425 g) black beans
- ½ cup (72 g) vital wheat gluten flour
- ¼ cup (60 ml) barbecue sauce
- 1 tablespoon (15 ml) liquid smoke
- ½ teaspoon black pepper
- 2 tablespoons (32 g) peanut butter

Directions

a) Reconstitute the TVP by mixing it with the water and soy sauce in a microwave-safe bowl, covering tightly with plastic wrap, and microwaving on high for 5 minutes. Alternatively, you can pour boiling water over the TVP and soy sauce, then cover and let stand for 10 minutes.

b) Add the beans, wheat gluten, ¼ cup (60 ml) barbecue sauce, liquid smoke, pepper, and peanut butter to the reconstituted TVP once it is cool enough to handle. Mush it together with your hands until it is uniform and most of the beans are mashed up.

c) Form into 6 patties.

d) Grill these babies up on the barbecue, brushing with the additional barbecue sauce as you go, about 5 minutes per side. Alternatively, these can be pan-fried in a bit of oil, then topped with additional barbecue sauce.

55.   Vegan Bacon patties

Ingredient

- 1 cup (100 g) TVP granules
- 2 tablespoons (30 ml) steak sauce
- 1 tablespoon (15 ml) liquid smoke
- ¼ cup (60 ml) canola oil
- 1/3 cup (85 g) peanut butter
- ½ cup (72 g) vital wheat gluten flour
- ½ cup (50 g) imitation bacon bits
- ¼ cup (30 g) nutritional yeast
- 1 tablespoon (7 g) paprika
- 1 tablespoon (6 g) garlic powder
- 1 teaspoon ground black pepper

Directions

a) Reconstitute the TVP by either mixing together the TVP, water, steak sauce, and liquid smoke in a microwave-safe bowl, covering tightly with plastic wrap, and microwaving on high for 5 minutes, or alternatively pour boiling water over the TVP, steak sauce, and liquid smoke, then cover and let stand for 10 minutes.

b) Add the oil and peanut butter to the TVP mixture. In a mixing bowl, mix together the wheat gluten, bacon bits, yeast, paprika, garlic powder, and black pepper.

c) Add the TVP mixture to the flour mixture and knead until well incorporated. Cover and let stand for 20 minutes.

d) Form into 4 to 6 patties and prepare as desired. If grilling, grill for 5 to 7 minutes per side.

56. Barley Oat patties

Yield: 6 Servings

Ingredient

- 1 cup Canned butter beans
- ¾ cup Bulgur; cooked
- ¾ cup Barley; cooked
- ½ cup Quick oatmeal; uncooked
- 1½ tablespoon Soy sauce
- 2 tablespoons Barbecue sauce
- 1 teaspoon Dried basil
- ½ cup Onions; finely chopped
- 1 Clove garlic; finely minced
- 1 Stalk celery; chopped
- 1 teaspoon Salt
- Pepper to taste

Directions

a) With a fork or potato masher, mash beans just slightly. They should be chunky, not pureed. Add the rest of the ingredients and form 6 patties.

b) Spray skillet with oil and brown patties on both sides.

57. Tempeh patties

Makes 4 burgers

Ingredient

- 8 ounces tempeh, cut into 1/2-inch dice
- ¾ cup chopped onion
- 2 garlic cloves, chopped
- ¾ cup chopped walnuts
- 1/2 cup old-fashioned or quick-cooking oats
- 1 tablespoon minced fresh parsley
- 1/2 teaspoon dried oregano
- 1/2 teaspoon dried thyme
- 1/2 teaspoon salt
- 1/4 teaspoon freshly ground black pepper
- 3 tablespoons olive oil
- Dijon mustard
- 4 whole grain burger rolls
- Sliced red onion, tomato, lettuce, and avocado

Directions

a) In a medium saucepan of simmering water, cook the tempeh for 30 minutes. Drain and set aside to cool.

b) In a food processor, combine the onion and garlic and process until minced. Add the cooled tempeh, the walnuts, oats, parsley, oregano, thyme, salt, and pepper. Process until well blended. Shape the mixture into 4 equal patties.

c) In a large skillet, heat the oil over medium heat. Add the burgers and cook until cooked thoroughly and browned on both sides, about 7 minutes per side.

d) Spread desired amount of mustard onto each half of the rolls and layer each roll with lettuce, tomato, red onion, and avocado, as desired. Serve immediately.

WRAPS AND ROLLS

58. No Bread Turkey Club

Ingredients

- 5-6 romaine lettuce leave
- 4 pieces of turkey lunch meat
- 3 strips of cooked bacon
- 1/4 of an avocado
- 3 slices of tomato
- Optional: a few teaspoons of your favorite sandwich spread

Directions

a) Lay a piece of parchment paper on a large plate or cutting board

b) Rinse and dry the romaine lettuce

c) Then cut the stems out of each piece of lettuce – you can skip this step, but I find it rolls easier without the stems

d) Lay the lettuce on the parchment in overlapping lines until you form a 10" x 8" rectangle of lettuce

e) Then drizzle on your sandwich spread of choice – I usually use ranch

f) Layer on your fillings starting with lunch meat, then bacon, then tomatoes, and finally avocado

g) Use the parchment to help roll the sandwich into a tight tube by folding in the ends as you roll

h) Slice the sandwich in half and fold down the parchment as you eat!

59. Collard Wraps with Quinoa and Sweet Potato

SERVINGS 4

Ingredients

- 1 medium (250g) sweet potato
- 2 teaspoon ground cumin divided
- 2 tablespoons olive oil divided
- salt and pepper
- ⅔ cup quinoa or 2 cups cooked
- 1 15 oz. (400g) can black beans drained and rinsed
- 3 tablespoon tahini
- zest and juice of 1 lemon
- 1 red bell pepper
- 8 large collard leaves

Directions

a) Preheat oven to 375°F/190 C.

b) Slice the sweet potato into ½" slices, then cut each slice into ½" strips. Toss with 1 tablespoon of the oil, 1 teaspoon of the cumin and salt and pepper.

c) Spread onto a baking sheet in a single layer and bake for 15 minutes or until cooked.

d) Cook the quinoa according to package instructions. Drain, rinse under cold water and add to a mixing bowl with the beans, tahini, lemon zest and juice and remaining oil and cumin. Toss to combine.

e) Bring a large pan of water to the boil. Prepare a large bowl of iced water.

f) Wash the leaves well, then trim each leaf across the broad part of the base. Hold the knife flat to the leaf, then run down gently to slice off the bulbous part of the stem so it lays flat.

g) Place the prepared leaves into the boiling water for 15 seconds to balance, then remove and place into the iced water until cool. Drain.

h) Slice the bell pepper into $\frac{1}{2}$ inch strips.

i) Lay a prepared leaf on the worktop and add 2-3 tablespoons of the quinoa mixture along the center. Add a few pieces each of pepper and sweet potato.

j) Fold two opposite edges into the middle over the filling, then fold a third side over. Roll towards the final edge to form a little wrap parcel, keep the seam on the bottom to keep them closed. Repeat with the remaining leaves and fillings.

60.   Copycat in N' Out Burger

Ingredients

Burgers:

- 1 lb. Ground Beef (80/20 preferred)
- Salt and Pepper
- 4 slices, Yellow American Cheese
- Sauce Ingredients:
- 1/3 cup Mayo (I like avocado mayo personally)
- 1 Tablespoons Sugar Free Ketchup or sub 1 Teaspoon Organic Tomato Paste
- 1 Teaspoon Mustard
- 2 Tablespoons Diced Pickles
- 1-2 teaspoons Pickle Juice
- 1/2 Teaspoon Salt
- 1/2 Teaspoon Paprika
- 1/2 teaspoons Garlic Powder

Toppings:

- Iceberg Lettuce "buns"
- Sliced tomato

Pickles

- 1/2 Yellow Onion, sliced thin (traditional in N' Out caramelizes the onions too)
- Optional - Smart Buns

Directions

a) Start by preparing the sauce. In a small bowl combine the mayo, sugar free ketchup, 1 teaspoons of mustard, diced pickles, pickle juice, and spices. Mix together and test taste. Flavors do meld better together over time so feel free to adjust.

b) To prep the hamburger patties, measure out 2 oz. of meat per patty and roll into a meatball. Repeat so you have 10 total meatballs. Season the tops with sea salt and cracked black pepper.

c) Preheat your cast iron/ griddle to a high heat. Add a little oil to the pan if necessary. Place two meatballs onto the griddle or pan, use a wide spatula and press down. I like to use a potato masher to help me press and smash the burgers as flat as possible. Baste the top (optional) in mustard before flipping. Work quickly. As the edges appear to brown, flip them. Place one piece of American cheese on one burger patty and stack the second patty over it.

d) To assemble, start with a bottom piece of lettuce, add the slice onion, the double stacked burger patty, tomato, pickles, and the sauce.

e) Cover with the second lettuce bun and dig in!

61. Carrot and Spinach Wrap

Ingredients

- 1 flour tortilla
- 2 heaped Tablespoons hummus
- a generous handful of fresh spinach
- 1 medium carrot
- 2 Tablespoons salted cashews

Directions

a) Peel your carrot, then grate coarsely.

b) Roughly chop the cashews.

c) Spread your tortilla with hummus, then lay the spinach across the middle of the wrap, top with the grated carrot and nuts.

d) To wrap your tortilla, fold in the sides, roll the top of the tortilla towards you wrapping it firmly around the filling, tucking in the edges as you go.

e) Cut your wrap in half and serve with a few crisps (chips) and some apple wedges, with some dressed salad or wrapped in foil if you are on the go.

62. Vegan Mediterranean Wraps

Ingredients

- 1 medium cucumber
- $\frac{1}{2}$ teaspoon (plus a couple pinches) of salt
- 1 medium tomato diced
- $\frac{1}{4}$ red onion diced
- $\frac{1}{4}$ green pepper diced
- 4 tablespoons chopped Kalamata olives
- 1 jar (540 grams / 19 oz..) chickpeas
- 200 grams (7 oz..) vegan yogurt
- 2 tablespoons chopped fresh dill
- 1 clove of garlic minced
- 1 tablespoon lemon juice
- 2 cups (112 grams) chopped lettuce
- 4 large tortillas

Directions

a) Combine the diced cucumber, tomato, red onion, green pepper, and black olives. Drain and rinse the chickpeas and put them in a bowl. Smash them with your hands or with a fork.

b) In a bowl combine the grated cucumber, vegan yogurt, dill, garlic, lemon juice and a pinch of salt and pepper. Add 3 tablespoons of the tzatziki along with $\frac{1}{2}$ teaspoon of salt and pepper. Mix well.

c) Make the wraps with a handful of lettuce, smashed chickpeas, mixed diced vegetables and a few dollops of tzatziki.

63.   Chickpea hummus wraps

Ingredients

- 1 ½ cups chickpeas
- 2 to 3 Tablespoons brine
- 1 small garlic clove
- 2 Tablespoons tahini
- 1 Tablespoon lemon juice
- ¼ teaspoon salt
- 1 ½ cups black beans 15-ounce can
- 4 to 6 whole wheat tortillas
- 2 cups cooked brown rice
- 2 cups chopped romaine lettuce
- ½ cup turnip pickles

Directions

a) Combine chickpeas, chickpea brine, garlic, tahini, lemon juice, and salt in a food processor.

b) Combine black beans, garlic, tahini, lemon juice, cumin, and salt in a food processor. Stop occasionally to scrape down the sides, until the hummus is completely creamy.

c) Warm tortillas in a dry skillet or grill pan on both sides on a medium heat, or warm them in the microwave for about 30 seconds.

d) Fill warmed tortillas with spoonful of rice, chickpea hummus, black bean hummus, romaine, and turnip pickles. Fold each wrap like a burrito.

64. Baby Beet Wraps

Ingredients

- 1 flour tortilla wrap
- 1 Tablespoons dairy-free pesto
- 15g/ 1 large handful rocket (arugula)
- 6 slices of cucumber
- 4 cherry tomatoes, halved
- 1 heaped Tablespoons sweet corn
- 3 baby beets

Directions

a) Spread the tortilla with the pesto, leaving a border around the edge. This makes it less messy as it's less likely to leak.

b) Top with rocket, cucumber and tomatoes on one side of the wrap, leaving a good space around the edge.

c) Pat the excess vinegar from the baby beets, halve and add to the wrap along with the sweet corn.

d) Wrap the sides of the wrap over the filling a little, lift the top of the wrap over and roll towards you.

e) Cut in half and serve.

65. Vegan Shawarma

Ingredients

- 1/3 cup (55g) Canned Chickpeas
- 2 Tablespoons Nutritional Yeast
- Spices
- 1 Tablespoons Soy Sauce
- 1/4 cup (65g) Tomato Paste
- 1/3 cup (80ml) Vegetable Stock
- 1 teaspoons Dijon Mustard
- 1/8 teaspoons Liquid Smoke
- 1 cup (150g) Vital Wheat Gluten
- Marinade
- 6 Wraps
- Shredded Lettuce

Directions

a) Add the chickpeas, nutritional yeast, spices, soy sauce, tomato paste, paprika, vegetable stock, Dijon mustard and liquid smoke to the food processor and process until well mixed.

b) Add the vital wheat gluten. Flatten it on a work surface and pat it down into the shape of a large steak. Steam

c) Mix up marinade and pour it over the seitan strips. Fry the seitan in the marinade,

d) Spread some spicy hummus to a pita bread or wrap. Add shredded lettuce and sliced cucumber and tomato into a wrap, top with a few seitan strips and finish with a dollop of vegan tzatziki.

66.   Chipotle Tofu Rainbow Wraps

Ingredients

- 14-ounce package extra-firm tofu
- 1/4 cup tahini
- 1/4 cup nutritional yeast
- 4 teaspoons liquid aminos
- 1 tablespoons apple cider vinegar
- 1/4-1/2 teaspoon salt, to taste
- Hummus Spread
- 2 tablespoons diced green onions
- 1 tablespoon Dijon mustard
- 2 cups chopped romaine lettuce
- 1 cup shredded red cabbage
- 1 cup peeled carrot ribbons
- 1 cup tomato slices, halved
- 1/2 cup thinly sliced red onion
- 1/2 cup sliced avocado

Directions

a) In a bowl, whisk tahini, yeast, water, liquid aminos, apple cider vinegar, chipotle, and salt, until combined. Add chopped tofu.

b) Transfer mixture to an air fryer basket, and spread out into a single layer. Cook at 400F for 20 minutes. Prepare the hummus sauce

c) Lay out one tortilla, and smear hummus in the center. Place 1/4 of the tofu on top, then 1/2 cup romaine, 1/4 cup cabbage, 1/4 cup carrots, 1/4 cup tomato slices, roughly 2 tablespoons red onion, and 2 tablespoons avocado.

67. Seared Portobello Fajitas

Makes 4 fajitas

Ingredients

- 2 tablespoons olive oil
- 3 large portobello mushroom caps, lightly rinsed, patted dry, and cut into 1/4-inch strips
- 1 serrano or other hot chile, seeded and minced (optional)
- 3 cups fresh baby spinach
- 1/4 teaspoon ground cumin
- 1/4 teaspoon dried oregano
- Salt and freshly ground black pepper
- 4 (10-inch) flour tortillas, warmed
- 1 cup tomato salsa

Directions

a) In a large skillet, heat the oil over medium-high heat. Add the mushrooms, onion, and chile, if using, and cook until seared on the outside and slightly softened, stirring occasionally about 5 minutes.

b) Add the spinach and cook until wilted, 1 to 2 minutes. Season with the cumin, oregano, salt, and pepper to taste.

c) To assemble the fajitas, place 1 tortilla on a work surface. Spread with one-quarter of the mushroom mixture. Spoon ¼ cup of the salsa on top and roll up tightly. Repeat with remaining ingredients. Serve immediately.

68. Beer-Marinated Seitan Fajitas

Makes 4 fajitas

Ingredients

- 1/2 cup chopped red onion
- 1 garlic clove, minced
- 1/2 cup beer
- 2 teaspoons fresh lime juice
- 1 tablespoon chopped fresh cilantro
- 1/4 teaspoon crushed red pepper
- 1/2 teaspoon salt
- 8 ounces seitan
- 2 tablespoons olive oil
- 1 ripe Hass avocado
- 4 (10-inch) flour tortillas, warmed
- 1/2 cup tomato salsa

Directions

a) In a shallow bowl, combine the onion, garlic, beer, lime juice, cilantro, crushed red pepper, and salt. Add the seitan and marinate for 4 hours or overnight in the refrigerator.

b) Remove the seitan from the marinade, reserving the marinade. In a large skillet, heat the oil over medium heat. Add the seitan and cook until browned on both sides, about 10 minutes. Add the reserved marinade and simmer until most of the liquid is evaporated.

c) Pit, peel, and cut the avocado into 1/2-inch slices. To assemble the fajitas, place 1 tortilla on a

d) work surface and top with one-quarter of the seitan strips, salsa, and avocado slices. Roll up tightly and repeat with the remaining ingredients. Serve immediately.

69.   Seitan Tacos

Makes 4 tacos

Ingredients

- 2 tablespoons olive oil
- 12 ounces seitan
- 2 tablespoons soy sauce
- 1 1/2 teaspoons chili powder
- 1/4 teaspoon ground cumin
- 1/4 teaspoon garlic powder
- 12 (6-inch) soft corn tortillas
- 1 ripe Hass avocado
- Shredded romaine lettuce
- 1 cup tomato salsa

Directions

a) In a large skillet, heat the oil over medium heat. Add the seitan and cook until browned, about 10 minutes. Sprinkle with the soy sauce, chili powder, cumin, and garlic powder, stirring to coat. Remove from heat.

b) Preheat the oven to 225°F. In a medium skillet, warm the tortillas over medium heat and stack them on a heatproof plate. Cover with foil and place them in the oven to keep them soft and warm.

c) Pit and peel the avocado and cut into 1/4-inch slices. Arrange the taco filling, avocado, and lettuce on a platter and serve along with the warmed tortillas, salsa, and any additional toppings.

70. Refried Bean and Salsa Quesadillas

Makes 4 quesadillas

Ingredients

- 1 tablespoon canola or grapeseed oil, plus more for frying
- 1 1/2 cups cooked or 1 (15.5-ounce) can pinto beans, drained and mashed
- 1 teaspoon chili powder
- 4 (10-inch) flour tortillas
- 1 cup tomato salsa

a) In a medium saucepan, heat the oil over medium heat. Add the mashed beans and chili powder and cook, stirring, until hot, about 5 minutes. Set aside.

b) To assemble, place 1 tortilla on a work surface and spoon about 1/4 cup of the beans across the

c) bottom half. Top the beans with the salsa and onion, if using. Fold the top half of the tortilla over the filling and press slightly.

d) In a large skillet heat a thin layer of oil over medium heat. Place folded quesadillas, 1 or 2 at a time, into the hot skillet and heat until hot, turning once, about 1 minute per side.

e) Cut quesadillas into 3 or 4 wedges and arrange them on plates. Serve immediately.

71. Spinach, Mushroom, and Black Bean Quesadillas

Makes 4 quesadillas

Ingredients

- 1 1/2 cups cooked or 1 (15.5 ounces) can of black beans, drained and rinsed
- 1 tablespoon olive oil
- 1/2 cup minced red onion
- 2 garlic cloves, minced
- 2 cups sliced white mushrooms
- 4 cups fresh baby spinach
- Salt and freshly ground black pepper
- 4 (10-inch) flour tortillas
- Canola or grapeseed oil, for frying

Directions

a) Place the black beans in a medium bowl and coarsely mash them. Set aside.

b) In a small skillet, heat the olive oil over medium heat. Add the onion and garlic and cover and cook until softened, about 5 minutes. Stir in the mushrooms and cook, uncovered, until softened. Add the spinach, season with salt and pepper to taste, and cook, stirring, until the spinach is wilted about 3 minutes.

c) Stir in the mashed black beans and continue cooking, stirring, until liquid is absorbed.

d) To assemble quesadillas, place 1 tortilla at a time on a work surface and spoon about one-quarter mixture onto the bottom half of the tortilla. Fold the top half of the tortillas over the filling and press lightly.

e) In a large skillet, heat a thin layer of oil over medium heat. Place the folded quesadillas, 1 or 2 at a time, into the hot skillet and heat over medium heat until hot, turning once, about 1 minute per side.

f) Cut the quesadillas into 3 or 4 wedges each and arrange them on plates. Serve immediately.

72. Black Bean and Corn Burritos

Makes 4 burritos

Ingredients

- 1 tablespoon olive oil
- 1/2 cup chopped onion
- 11/2 cups cooked or 1 (15.5-ounce) can of black beans, drained and rinsed
- 1/2 cup tomato salsa
- 4 (10-inch) flour tortillas, warmed

Directions

a) In a saucepan, heat the oil over medium heat. Add the onion, cover, and cook until softened, about 5 minutes. Add the beans and mash them until broken up.

b) Add the corn and salsa, stirring to combine. Simmer, stirring, until the bean mixture is hot about 5 minutes.

c) To assemble burritos, place 1 tortilla on a work surface and spoon about 1/2 cup of the filling

d) mixture down the center. Roll up tightly, tucking in the sides. Repeat with the remaining ingredients. Serve seam side down.

73. Red Bean Burritos

Makes 4 burritos

Ingredients

- 1 tablespoon olive oil
- 1 medium onion, chopped
- 1 medium red bell pepper, chopped
- 1 1/2 cups cooked or 1 (15.5-ounce) can of dark red kidney beans, drained and rinsed
- 1 cup tomato salsa
- 4 (10-inch) flour tortillas, warmed
- 1 cup hot cooked rice
- 1 ripe Hass avocado, pitted, peeled, and cut into 1/4-inch slices

Directions

a) In a medium saucepan, heat the oil over medium heat. Add the onion and bell pepper, cover, and cook until softened, about 5 minutes. Add the beans and salsa and cook, stirring to combine. Simmer, mashing the beans as you stir them, until hot.

b) To assemble burritos, place 1 tortilla on a work surface and spoon about 1/2 cup of the bean

c) mixture down the center. Top with the rice, followed by slices of avocado and extra salsa, if desired. Roll up tightly, tucking in the sides. Repeat with the remaining ingredients. Serve seam-side down.

74.   Ham and cheese cucumber roll ups

Ingredients

Avocado-hummus spread

- 1 ripe avocado, pitted
- 2 Tablespoons plain hummus
- 1 garlic clove, pressed
- 2 Teaspoon fresh lime juice
- kosher salt and fresh black pepper, to taste

Roll-ups

- 1-2 seedless cucumbers, ends removed
- 6-8 slices Honey Deli Ham
- 6 slices deli provolone cheese
- fresh chopped cilantro
- fresh baby spinach leaves

Directions

Avocado-hummus spread

a) In a small bowl, mash the avocado flesh with a fork. To the avocado, add hummus, garlic, and lime juice. Season with salt and pepper, to taste. Mix until well blended.

Roll-ups

b) With a mandolin slicer, slice the cucumber into thin strips. I was able to get about 10 strips out of one medium size cucumber. First couple or so strips were too small to use so I tossed those for a salad. You may have little less or more strips depending on the size of cucumber.

c) Place 5 cucumber strips next to each other, on a paper lined flat surface, such as a cutting board, and using a clean paper towel, blot some of the moisture on top.

d) Spread 2-3 tablespoons of the avocado-hummus evenly over the slices. Then add 3-4 slices of ham, 3 slices of provolone cheese, light layer of cilantro leaves, and light layer of baby spinach.

e) Starting at one end, tightly roll all of the cucumber slices into one long "sushi" roll.

f) Using a sharp knife, cut the roll into individual servings. Secure with a toothpick and place on a serving platter. Repeat with the remaining cucumber strips.

g) These are best when served same day. I was able to get about 10 roll-ups out of one cucumber.

75. Crispy Salami Roll-ups

Makes 12

Ingredients

- 250g cream cheese
- 2 Tablespoons (23g) capers, drained and chopped
- 1 Tablespoons (5g) finely chopped basil
- 12 rounds Hungarian salami (276g)

Directions:

a) In a small bowl mix together cream cheese, capers and basil.

b) Season with cracked pepper.

c) Lay the salami onto a clean surface and spread a generous tablespoon of mixture across each.

d) Roll up across itself and place seam side down into the air fryer basket.

e) Cook at 180°C, for 7 minutes.

76. Italian Beef Wrappers

SERVINGS 4

Ingredients

- 1 Teaspoon Olive Oil
- 1/2 cup Green bell pepper, cut into strips
- 1/2 cup onion, cut into strips
- 1/2 pepperoncini, thinly sliced
- 1/2 Teaspoon Italian seasoning
- 8 slices Deli Italian beef, 1/8" thick
- 8 String Cheese Sticks

Directions

a) In a medium skillet, heat the oil over medium heat. Combine the olive oil and the following four ingredients in a mixing bowl. Cook for 3-4 minutes, or until crisp tender.

b) Place the mixture on a platter and set aside for 15 minutes to cool.

c) How to Put It Together: On a cutting board, lay four slices of Italian beef flat. Place 1 string cheese stick in the center of each piece of meat, crosswise.

d) Add part of the pepper and onion mixture on the top. Fold one side of the beef slice over the cheese and veggie mixture, then wrap up, seam side down.

e) Assemble the roll-ups on a serving platter.

77. Italian Pepperoni Roll-ups

Servings 35

Ingredients

- 5 10" flour tortillas
- 16 ounces cream cheese softened
- 2 teaspoons minced garlic
- 1/2 cup sour cream
- 1/2 cup Parmesan cheese
- 1/2 cup Italian shredded cheese or mozzarella cheese
- 2 teaspoons Italian seasoning
- 16 ounces pepperoni slices
- 3/4 cup finely chopped yellow and orange peppers
- 1/2 cup finely chopped fresh mushrooms

Directions

a) In a mixing basin, beat the cream cheese until smooth. Combine the garlic, sour cream, cheeses, and Italian seasoning in a mixing bowl. Mix until everything is well blended.

b) Spread the mixture evenly among the 5 flour tortillas. Cover the entire tortilla with the cheese mixture.

c) Place a pepperoni layer on top of the cheese mixture.

d) Overlap the pepperoni with the coarsely sliced peppers and mushrooms.

e) Tightly roll each tortilla and wrap it in plastic wrap.

f) Set aside for at least 2 hours in the refrigerator.

78. Appetizer Tortilla Pinwheels

Ingredients

- 1 package (8 ounces) cream cheese, softened
- 1 cup shredded cheddar cheese
- 1 cup sour cream
- 1 can (4-1/4 ounces) chopped ripe olives
- 1 can (4 ounces) chopped green chiles, well drained
- 1/2 cup chopped green onions
- Garlic powder to taste
- Seasoned salt to taste
- 5 flour tortillas (10 inches)
- Salsa, optional

Directions

a) Beat cream cheese, cheese and sour cream until blended. Stir in olives, green chiles, green onions and seasonings.

b) Spread over tortillas; roll up tightly. Wrap each in plastic, twisting ends to seal; refrigerate several hours.

c) Unwrap. Cut into 1/2- to 3/4-in. slices, using a serrated knife. If desired, serve with salsa.

79. Crispy vegan rolls

Yield: 24 Servings

Ingredients

- 5 Carrots, cooked
- Salt
- 1 Stalk celery; chopped fine and cooked
- Peanut or vegetable oil
- Sesame oil
- 3 large Onions; chopped fine
- 2 Green onions; sliced thin
- 3 Red bell peppers; chopped fine
- 20 Shiitake mushrooms; chopped fine
- 1 bunch Cilantro leaves; chopped
- 1 pack Spring roll wrappers; (11oz.)
- 1 tablespoon Cornstarch

Directions

a) Put 2 teaspoons peanut oil and 2 teaspoons sesame oil in large heated skillet. add chopped onions, sliced green onions and bell peppers. Toss in mushrooms and cook 2 to 3 minutes.

b) Add carrots, celery and cilantro and stir. Season to taste with salt and pepper

c) Position 1 wrapper. Brush beaten egg on top corner. Arrange ⅓ cup filling mixture in line 2 inches from bottom corner. Wrap corner over mixture and pull back to tighten.

d) Fold over two sides and roll to end of wrapper. Fry

80. Vegan stuffed cabbage rolls

Ingredients

- 1 large frozen Cabbage, thawed
- 2 tablespoons Oil
- 1 Onion, diced
- 1 Stalk celery, diced
- 2 tablespoons Diced green pepper
- 2 tablespoons Flour
- 1 46-oz. can tomato juice
- 4 tablespoons Tomato paste
- ½ cup Sugar
- Dash Salt, Paprika, Curry powder
- 2 cups Cooked rice
- 2 Bay leaves
- 1 large Apple, peeled and diced
- ¼ cup Golden raisins

Directions

a) In a skillet, heat the oil and add the onion, celery and green pepper. Mix in the seasoning. Add vegetables to rice and mix well. Set aside.

b) Heat the oil. Stir in the flour and cook until brown. Add remaining sauce ingredients Add the cabbage rolls carefully, placing them in the sauce one at a time. Cook for 2 hours.

c) Place a tablespoon of filling on the rib of the leaf, near the base. Fold the base of the leaf over the filling and roll once. Fold sides toward the center to enclose and make straight edges.

81. Vegan nori rolls

Yield: 1 Serving

Ingredients

- ¼ cup Soy sauce
- 2 teaspoons Honey
- 1 teaspoon Minced garlic
- 1 tablespoon Grated ginger root
- 1 pounds Extra-firm tofu or tempeh
- 2 tablespoons Rice vinegar
- 1 tablespoon Superfine sugar
- 2 cups Cooked short grain brown rice
- 2 Scallions minced, white part only
- 2 tablespoons Toasted sesame seeds
- 5 Sheets nori
- 1 cup Finely shredded carrots
- 10 Fresh spinach leaves, steamed
- 1½ cup Alfalfa sprouts

Directions

a) Combine soy sauce, honey, garlic and ginger. Add tofu or tempeh; marinate at least 30 minutes.

b) Combine rice vinegar and sugar. Add rice and Stir in scallions and sesame seeds; mix well.

c) Place a sheet of nori on waxed paper. spoon mixture in center of nori. Fold

82. Mediterranean Rolls

Ingredients

For the wraps:

- 1¼ cups (156 g) all-purpose flour
- ¼ teaspoon salt
- ¼ teaspoon baking powder
- ¼ teaspoon baking soda
- ½ teaspoon garlic powder
- ½ teaspoon dried basil
- ½ cup (120 ml) water
- 6 ounces (168 g) extra-firm tofu,
- ¼ cup (40 g) sun-dried tomatoes
- 1 teaspoon garlic powder
- 1 teaspoon onion powder
- 2 tablespoons (15 g) nutritional yeast
- ½ teaspoon paprika
- 1 tablespoon (15 ml) extra-virgin olive oil

Directions

a) Mix together the flour, salt, baking powder, baking soda, garlic powder, onion powder, parsley, and basil. Add the water and knead until a nice elastic dough ball forms. On a well-floured surface, roll each piece flat.

b) Combine all the filling ingredients in a bowl and stir until very well incorporated. place one portion of the filling in the center of one wrap and roll it up like a little burrito.

c) Place on the baking sheet. Bake for 15 to 20 minutes.

83.   Avocado Spring Rolls

Ingredients

- 12 large rice spring roll wrappers
- 6 ounces (168 g) baby spinach leaves
- 1 cucumber, seeded and cut
- 3 avocados, peeled and sliced
- 2 to 3 cups shredded carrots
- 6 ounces prepared rice stick noodles

Directions

a) On an ample flat surface, preferably near the stove, prepare a workstation. Have at hand a shallow pan of hot, but not boiling, water, the rice wrappers, the spinach leaves, the cucumber matchsticks, the sliced avocados, the shredded carrots, and the prepared noodles.

b) Place a damp dish towel on the flat surface closest to you. Carefully place one rice wrapper in the hot water for about 10 seconds, or until it is soft and pliable. Lay the wrapper flat on the dish towel.

c) Start by placing a small amount of spinach, about 5 leaves, onto the wrapper, then layer on the cucumber, avocado, carrot, and finally a small handful of noodles. Roll up tightly like a tiny burrito.

84. Vegetarian Spring Roll

Ingredients

- Vegetable Platter
- 8 ounces Thin rice vermicelli
- Peanut sauce
- 1-ounce Cellophane noodles
- 1 tablespoon mushrooms
- 6 Dried Chinese mushrooms
- 1 large Carrot, finely shredded
- 1 large Leek, white part only, chopped
- 6 Water chestnuts
- 1 pounds Firm bean curd (tofu), crumbled
- 1 cup Fresh bean sprouts
- 6 Garlic cloves, minced
- 3 tablespoons Nuoc mam
- 2 Eggs
- ½ cup Sugar
- 40 smalls Rounds of rice papers

Directions

a) Prepare the Vegetable Platter, noodles and dipping sauce. Set aside.

b) Combine all of the filling ingredients in a large mixing bowl; blend well with your hands. Set aside.

c) Assemble the rolls: Fill a large bowl with 4 cups of warm water and dissolve the sugar in it.

d) To serve, each diner wraps a roll in a lettuce leaf along with some noodles and selected items from the Vegetable Platter and dips the package in the dipping sauce.

85. Vegetarian cabbage rolls

Yield: 12 servings

Ingredients

- 2 each Cabbage head
- ¾ cup Barley, uncooked
- ¾ cup Bulgur, uncooked
- 1 cup Rice, uncooked
- 1 large Onions
- 2 cups Prego
- 4 Garlic cloves, crushed
- ½ cup Pine nuts
- 10½ ounce Tofu, firm
- ½ bunch Parsley; chopped
- 6 tablespoons Sauce, soy
- 4 tablespoons Molasses
- Seasoning
- 4½ tablespoon Vinegar, wine

Directions

a) Filling: Precook grains in water until done. Crush tofu. Sauté remaining ingredients in oil until cooked and add cooked grains.

b) Cabbage: Core cabbage and cook in boiling water for several minutes.

c) Pull leaves away as they soften. Cut out hard core of leaf. Cut largest leaves in half.

d) Fill cabbage leaves with cooked filling and wrap, tucking sides and ends in to form neat rolls. Place rolls snugly in casserole against each other. Spoon remaining sauce over.

e) Cover tightly and bake 2 hours. Leave in oven until serving time.

86.   Vegetarian egg rolls

Ingredients

- 1 pack Egg roll wrappers
- Sesame oil
- 1 cup Celery, finely chopped
- 1 Onion, small, finely chopped
- 2 Garlic cloves, minced
- 1 cup Cabbage, finely shredded
- 1 cup Mushroom, finely chopped
- 1 Green pepper, finely chopped
- $\frac{1}{2}$ cup Water chestnuts, finely chop
- 1 cup Sprouts, bean or seed, fresh
- $\frac{1}{4}$ cup Soybeans, cooked and pureed
- 3 tablespoons Soy sauce
- $2\frac{1}{2}$ cup Brown rice, cooked

Directions

a) In a wok or frying pan sauté the vegetables in sesame oil in the order given. Add the remaining vegetables quickly. Stir the pureed soybeans and soy sauce together.

b) Place about $\frac{1}{4}$ cup filling in the center of each pancake or egg roll wrapper; fold the corners over envelope-style and seal with a flour-water paste.

c) Heat a large frying pan with oil in the bottom. Fry the rolls until they are crisp and brown, turning only once.

87. Vegetarian Thai spring rolls

Yield: 30 rolls

Ingredients

- 12 ounces Tofu
- 5 each Dried shiitake mushrooms,
- ¼ pounds Green beans
- 1 each Celery stalk
- ½ medium Carrot
- 2 each Green onions
- 3 tablespoons Vegetable oil
- 1 tablespoon Garlic, chopped
- ½ teaspoon Pepper
- 2 tablespoons Red curry paste
- 2 tablespoons Soy sauce
- 30 each Spring roll wrappers
- 3 cups Vegetable oil, for deep frying

Directions

a) Cut the tofu, mushrooms, beans, celery and carrot into large julienne slices. Chop the green onions. Set aside.

b) Put the 3 Tablespoons vegetable oil into a wok over medium heat. Stir-fry the garlic until it begins to brown. Add the soy sauce, tofu and all the vegetables except the green onions.

c) Separate the roll wrappers. Place the wrapper with the narrow side facing you. Place a scant $\frac{1}{4}$ c filling. Fold the closest edge to you over the filling, fold over the left and right edges and then roll.

d) Heat the oil for deep frying in a wok until hot. Deep-fry the rolls on each side until golden.

88. Unstuffed cabbage rolls

Yield: 4-6 serving

Ingredients

- ½ Head cabbage
- 2 cups Cooked rice
- ½ cup Whole wheat couscous
- ¼ cup Raisins
- ½ cup Fresh or frozen corn
- 1 can (16 oz.) chopped tomatoes
- 1 can (12 oz.) tomato sauce
- 1 teaspoon Fresh lemon juice
- 1 tablespoon Brown sugar
- Seasoning

Directions

a) Slice cabbage diagonally. Pour hot water over it to make it limp. Drain.

b) Mix rice, couscous, raisins and corn and set aside. Mix tomatoes with other ingredients and spread in bottom of a large ceramic casserole dish lightly coated with non-stick spray.

c) Cover with layers of the cabbage and the rice mixture. Top with the rest of the tomato mixture and cover with foil. Bake at 325 degrees F for 30-45 minutes, until bubbly. Serve hot.

89. Vegetarian summer roll

Yield: 6 servings

Ingredients

- 2 Limes; juiced
- Segments of 1 lime
- 1 tablespoon Dijon mustard
- 1 tablespoon Brown sugar
- ¼ cup Grape seed oil
- ¼ cup Thai basil leaves; whole
- ½ pounds Bean sprouts; hair removed
- 1 medium Red bell pepper; julienned
- 1 medium Carrot; peeled, julienned
- 1 pack Smoked tofu or tempeh
- 1 pack Rice papers
- Salt; to taste
- Freshly-ground black pepper; to taste

Directions

a) In a bowl whisk together juice, lime, mustard and sugar. Whisk in the oil and season. Toss with all the vegetables and tofu. Check for seasoning.

b) Lay out 1 wrapper and place a small mound of mix near the bottom. Roll bottom towards the middle. Fold in both sides and continue rolling. Finish roll and let rest. Individually wrap each roll with plastic wrap. Will hold for 2 hours in the fridge

90. Curried Tofu "Egg Salad" Pitas

Makes 4 sandwiches

Ingredients

- 1-pound extra-firm tofu drained and patted dry
- 1/2 cup vegan mayonnaise
- 1/4 cup chopped mango chutney
- 2 teaspoons Dijon mustard
- 1 tablespoon hot or mild curry powder
- 1 teaspoon salt
- 1/8 teaspoon ground cayenne
- 1 cup shredded carrots
- 2 celery ribs, minced
- 1/4 cup minced red onion
- 8 small Boston or other soft lettuce leaves
- 4 (7-inch) whole-wheat pitas, halved

Directions

a) Crumble the tofu and place it in a large bowl. Add the mayonnaise, chutney, mustard, curry powder, salt, and cayenne, and stir well until thoroughly mixed.

b) Add the carrots, celery, and onion and stir to combine. Refrigerate for 30 minutes to allow the flavors to blend.

c) Tuck a lettuce leaf inside each pita pocket, spoon some tofu mixture on top of the lettuce and serve.

SANDWICH/BURGER SPREADS

91. Sun-dried tomatoes Spread

Ingredients

- 2 tablespoons precooked big white beans
- 1/2 cup walnuts
- 10 slices of sun-dried tomatoes
- 1 tablespoon olive oil or other oil by choice
- 2 tablespoons pumpkin seeds
- 1 garlic clove
- Fresh basil, herbal salt and pepper, or other spices of your choice

Directions

Combine ingredients in a blender and blend until smooth and creamy.

92. Hummus dreams

Ingredients

- One cup of precooked chickpeas
- 1/2 cup walnuts
- One teaspoon of tahini (sesame paste)
- One teaspoon cumin
- One teaspoon of white wine vinegar
- Salt and pepper
- Fresh asparagus to use as a topping

Directions

Combine ingredients in a blender and blend until smooth and creamy.

93. Avocado love

Ingredients

- 1 avocado
- 2 Tablespoons freshly squeezed lemon juice
- Salt and pepper
- A pinch of black salt for a taste of egg (optional)

Directions

Combine ingredients in a blender and blend until smooth and creamy.

94. Pimiento spread for sandwich filling

Yield: 2 servings

Ingredient

- ½ cup Tofu
- 2 tablespoons Oil
- 2 tablespoons Apple cider vinegar
- 1 tablespoon Sugar
- 1½ teaspoon Salt
- ⅛ teaspoon Black pepper
- pinch garlic powder
- 1-pound firm tofu; crumbled
- 3 tablespoons Sweet pickle relish
- ½ cup Pimientos; drained and chopped

Directions

a) Combine the first 7 ingredients in a blender and blend until smooth and creamy.

b) Combine in a bowl with the remaining ingredients. Best if refrigerated overnight.

95.   Tofu sandwich spread

Yield: 4 servings

Ingredient

- 10 ounces firm tofu
- ½ Green bell pepper; diced
- 1 Stalk celery; diced
- 1 Carrot; grated
- 4 smalls Green onions; sliced
- 1 tablespoon Parsley
- 1 tablespoon capers
- 2 tablespoons Tofu based mayonnaise substitute
- 1 tablespoon prepared mustard
- ½ teaspoon Fresh lemon juice
- ¼ teaspoon Pepper
- ¼ teaspoon Thyme

Directions

a) Mix all ingredients and serve on your favorite bread with sprouts, tomatoes, and cucumbers.

96.   Veggie sandwich spread

Yield: 1 serving

Ingredient

- 1 pack of Firm tofu
- ½ cup Soy mayonnaise
- 1 each Green onion, diced
- 1 each Green bell pepper, diced
- 1 each Celery stalk, chopped
- ¼ cup Sunflower or sesame seeds
- 1 tablespoon Soy sauce
- 1 teaspoon Curry powder
- 1 teaspoon Turmeric
- 1 teaspoon Garlic powder

Directions

a) Crumble the tofu with a fork. Add remaining ingredients and mix well.

b) Serve on crackers or bread.

97. Easy "Tofuna" Sandwich Spread

Ingredients

- 8-ounce package of baked tofu (see note)
- 1/2 cup vegan mayonnaise, or as desired
- 1 large celery stalk, finely diced
- 1 scallion (green part only), thinly sliced
- 2 tablespoons nutritional yeast

Directions

a) Using your hands, crumble the tofu finely into a mixing bowl. Or, you can break the tofu into a few pieces, place it in a food processor, and pulse it on and off until finely and evenly chopped, then transfer it to a mixing bowl.

b) Add the mayonnaise and celery. Mix thoroughly. Stir in either or both of the optional ingredients. Transfer to a smaller serving container or serve straight from the mixing bowl.

98.   Indian lentil spread

Yield: 2 servings

Ingredient

- 1 cup cooked lentils
- 4 Cloves Garlic; pressed
- 2 teaspoons ground coriander
- 1 teaspoon ground cumin
- ½ teaspoon Ground turmeric
- ½ teaspoon Chili powder
- ½ teaspoon Ground ginger

Directions

a) Combine all of the ingredients in a small saucepan.

b) Cook gently over low heat, stirring occasionally, for 5 minutes, to allow the flavors to blend.

c) Chill for 1 hour.

99. Chickpea sandwich spread

Yield: 4 servings

Ingredient

- 1 cup Chickpeas; cooked
- Garlic powder to taste
- 3 tablespoons Italian salad dressing
- Salt and pepper to taste

Directions

a) Mash chickpeas with a fork and add seasonings.

b) Serve on toasted whole wheat bread with lettuce and tomato slices.

100. Curried bean spread

Yield: 8 servings

Ingredient

- ¾ cup Water
- 1 Onion; finely chopped
- 1 cup diced celery
- 1 green bell pepper; diced
- ½ cup Diced carrot
- 2 Cloves Garlic; minced
- 2½ teaspoon Curry powder
- ½ teaspoon Ground cumin
- 1 tablespoon Soy sauce
- 3 cups cooked white beans

Directions

a) Place the water in a saucepan and add all of the vegetables and the garlic.

b) Cook, stirring occasionally, for 15 minutes. Stir in the curry powder, cumin, and soy sauce, and mix well. Remove from the heat. Add the beans; mix well. Place the mixture in a food processor or blender and process briefly until chopped but not pureed. Chill.

CONCLUSION

Who says you need bread for a sandwich or a burger?

Whether you are gluten-free, Paleo, or just simply dislike bread these are the best sandwiches for you!